Routledge Revivals

India

Originally published in 1949, *India* does not attempt to provide a full history of the country, rather it brings to life the Indian story at the time by relating the position at the time of the new Indian Dominions to their historical background, and on the other hand, to concentrate attention on the political and economic growth of India, and to refer to other aspects when necessary. Therefore, it deals with the political and social legacy of ancient Hindu India and of medieval Muslim India in one chapter at the beginning, and the remainder of the volume is given to the description of the establishment and extension of European political rule and of the Indian reaction to it. Later chapters are concerned especially with India's struggle for independence and the difficult transition which culminated in the Partition.

India

C. H. Philips

Routledge
Taylor & Francis Group

First published in 1949
by Hutchinson's University Library

This edition first published in 2025 by Routledge
4 Park Square, Milton Park, Abingdon, Oxon, OX14 4RN

and by Routledge
605 Third Avenue, New York, NY 10017

Routledge is an imprint of the Taylor & Francis Group, an informa business

© 1949 C. H. Philips

Publisher's Note
The publisher has gone to great lengths to ensure the quality of this reprint but points out that some imperfections in the original copies may be apparent.

Disclaimer
The publisher has made every effort to trace copyright holders and welcomes correspondence from those they have been unable to contact.

A Library of Congress record exists under LCCN: 49049721

ISBN: 978-1-032-90461-0 (hbk)
ISBN: 978-1-003-55820-0 (ebk)
ISBN: 978-1-032-90466-5 (pbk)

Book DOI 10.4324/9781003558200

INDIA

by

C. H. PHILIPS

PROFESSOR OF ORIENTAL HISTORY
IN THE UNIVERSITY OF LONDON

HUTCHINSON'S UNIVERSITY LIBRARY
11 Stratford Place, London, W.1.

New York　　　*Melbourne*　　　*Sydney*　　　*Cape Town*

THIS VOLUME IS NUMBER 16 IN
HUTCHINSON'S UNIVERSITY LIBRARY

*Printed in Great Britain
at the Gainsborough Press, St. Albans,
by Fisher, Knight and Co. Ltd.*

CONTENTS

LIST OF MAPS

INTRODUCTION

HISTORY does not, indeed cannot, take account of all that happens. Not all the hopes and achievements, certainly not all the crimes, follies and misfortunes of mankind are recorded. Moreover, in a small book such as this dealing with a vast country like India, whose history extends over thousands of years, a place cannot even be found for all the relevant facts which have been recorded. Indeed, on this occasion it is only a week-end bag we are packing, not even a travelling trunk, and we cannot take everything with us.

Therefore, I have had to draw my limits and select my themes carefully, seeking no more than, on the one hand, to bring to life the Indian story by relating the present position of the new Indian Dominions to their historical background, and, on the other hand, to concentrate attention on the political and economic growth of India, and to refer to other aspects of her life only in so far as is essential to these main purposes.

With these limitations in mind, it becomes possible to deal with the political and social legacy of ancient Hindu India and of medieval Muslim India in one chapter at the beginning, and to give the remainder of the volume to the description of the establishment and extension of European political rule and of the fierce nationalist reactions thereby provoked in the hearts and minds of Indians. The later chapters are concerned especially with India's struggle for independence and with her difficult transition through turmoil and suffering from despotic to popular rule, which culminated in the Partition.

The bulk of this book was written in December, 1946, that is, before the Partition of India was decided on and eight months before it was carried out. Chapter VI on the Partition itself and slight consequential amendments to the other chapters were added in August, 1947.

I have used the general term "India" to describe the subcontinent as a whole, and the particular terms "Pakistan," "Dominion of India" or "Union of India" in reference to the two new Dominions.

C. H. PHILIPS.

School of Oriental and African Studies.

March 5, 1948.

CHAPTER I

THE HINDU AND MUSLIM LEGACY

I. INDIA TO-DAY

T w o world wars have brought to the continent of India much material prosperity and an increasing industrialization but she still remains, in terms of her population, largely agricultural and wretchedly poor. Seven out of ten Indians still earn their living directly from the soil and whereas, for example, in 1931 Britain's yearly income per head amounted to £73 10s., India's did not exceed £5. Where poverty leads, other great evils follow, in particular a population mounting so rapidly that it has almost doubled itself in seventy years and is at present increasing by some six millions annually, that is by sixteen thousand a day. Every minute there are eleven or twelve more Indian mouths to be fed! The numbers increase despite widespread disease and a death rate which gives the Indian at birth an expectation of life of no more than 26 years.

Adequately to feed, clothe and house her peoples, India must greatly expand her productive capacity per head, and at the same time exercise some check on the rate of growth of her population. The former demands an agricultural and industrial revolution, the latter depends on a wide diffusion of methods of birth control; and both taken together imply the existence of a literate population. Yet only twelve per cent of Indians can read and write.

In whichever direction one pursues India's problems the vicious circle appears to be complete.

A man may remain poor and yet find his soul, but not so a nation, for the interacting miseries of the people engender too many hatreds. Clearly no major change for the better in any of the main aspects of India's life can be achieved within a measurable span of time without a large-scale economic revolution, bringing with it a rapid and universal rise in the standard of living; and such a policy could be effectively carried through only with the full and continued support of the mass of public opinion. An alien government like the British, for example, could never hope to achieve this, and it remains to be seen whether Indian Governments, working in harmony or at cross purposes, can succeed where Britain failed. Therefore, at the heart of Indian difficulties to-day still lies, as for a generation past, the political problem.

To the western world Indian politics appear remote, complex and confusing, yet the essentials stand out boldly enough. Hindu-Muslim rivalry dominates the scene, not merely the religious antagonisms of ignorant peasants, but rather the clash of educated, clamant, middle-class groups, numbering altogether not more than one-tenth of the total population of some four hundred millions. These groups clearly perceive, in terms of power, place and employment, the stark realities of the political struggle.

On the one side, there stands the Indian National Congress, forged into one of the largest political organizations in the world by the genius of a unique political figure, Mahatma Gandhi, and now led by the forthright Jawaharlal Nehru. Claiming to be a truly national body and representative of all Indian groups, yet clearly drawing its main strength and inspiration from the caste Hindus who constitute over one-half of the total population, it has long sought to dominate a united India. Over against the Congress presses the All India Muslim League, representing the great proportion of the one hundred millions of Indian Muslims.

Under their single minded "Great Leader", Muhammad Ali Jinnah, they have maintained that Hindus and Muslims form separate nations and that the governments and the land must accordingly be divided. From the clash of these groups has emerged a partitioned India, on the one hand a Congress-dominated union of provinces—known as the Dominion of India—allied with a number of Princes' states, on the other hand a Muslim majority Dominion of Pakistan. Determined not to be entirely swallowed up by these leviathans the leaders of smaller minorities also raise their voices, particularly those of the four million warrior Sikhs concentrated in the heart of the newly partitioned Punjab, and of the widely dispersed forty to fifty millions of downtrodden, pathetically poor, outcaste Hindus—

scheduled castes, depressed classes, untouchables, as they are variously called—who have tended in the past to look for support, though not always leadership, to the Congress.

In the background, uneasily watching the struggle for power between these groups, stand the Indian Princes, some five to six hundred in number, who have ruled more or less autocratically over a quarter of India's peoples. Their extensive territories, so scattered that the political map of India looks like a patchwork quilt, cover two-fifths of the land and lie athwart many of the main lines of communication. The Princes appreciate that they must in future associate more closely with each other and with the new Dominions, but see no good reason why they should accept an inferior status.

Beside all groups, and responsible in some measure for the existence and even future of each, is Britain, who with much sacrifice had created and striven unsuccessfully to preserve an outward Indian unity.

To piece together this political jig-saw and to follow the undoubtedly tortuous course of Indian politics leading to the partition of India, we need first to understand the Indian environment which has profoundly conditioned the character and life of all her peoples and governments : then we must appreciate the influence of her early civilizations, which in her present day politics speak so loudly, on the one hand the Hindu culture forming a unique and awe-inspiring survival of the very remote past, and on the other the Islamic creed, which cleft India in two.

2. THE GEOGRAPHY BEHIND HISTORY

In shape India is like an enormous diamond, pointed to the north and south, the two northernmost edges formed by the Himalaya mountains, the mightiest and highest mountain ranges in the world and a bulwark tending throughout her long history to isolate India from Central Asia. Even to-day they constitute an effective barrier to a modern army. The southern point of the diamond juts into the great Indian Ocean, giving India the dominant position in those waters and linking her with Persia, Arabia, and Africa on the west and with Burma,

South-east Asia and the archipelago and Australia on the east: the strategic centre of a quarter of the world.

India is geographically compact, for comparison smaller than Soviet Russia and about three-fifths of the size of the United States ; an area of over 2,000,000 square miles into which you could comfortably tuck the whole of Europe proper and still leave room for another England or two. To cross the breadth of Britain by train from London to Liverpool you must travel 200 miles, to traverse India from Calcutta to Bombay you have to cover well over 1,200 miles. England's longest river, the Thames, winds 215 miles from its source; India's Ganges flows 1,680 miles to the sea. With such distances, and in a country where, until recent times, the normal speed of travel was that of the bullock cart, say at best three miles an hour, the land seems to stretch endlessly, giving to life a sense of timelessness which still remains the birthright of the Indian, and the source of his deepest feelings and philosophies.

India's climate, with its pronounced monotonous rhythm and suspended threat of overwhelming disaster, reinforces the influence of its geography. Much though not all of India lies within the tropics and the land is sunbaked. Life is given to it by two regular seasonal winds or monsoons, the first of which from the south-west passes over the warm ocean before striking across India about the beginning of June. By the end of September this monsoon begins to retreat and by the beginning of January the second, the north-east monsoon from the land, is blowing steadily over India. The south-west monsoon provides the bulk of India's rain, and the north-east monsoon waters in particular the northern plains of the Punjab and the Madras coast. Partial failure in any area of either monsoon, a frequent happening in India's history, means famine, pestilence and death. A monotonously scorching sun may encourage qualities of endurance but hardly of liveliness or of curiosity; disasters which can be faced and overcome may make a man resourceful, but India's climatic disasters, when they occur, are usually overwhelming. Under these conditions of climatic certainty and monotony varied by occasional devastating catastrophe, it is understandable that at the heart of India's two major religions, Hinduism and Islam, should grow a sombre

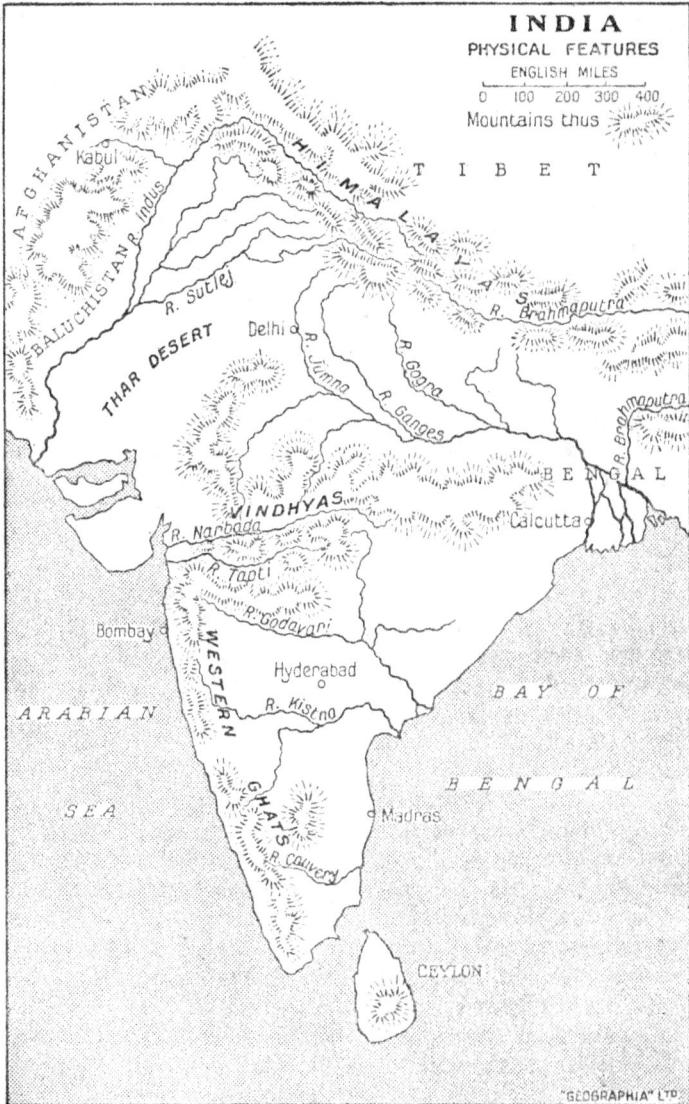

INDIA
PHYSICAL FEATURES
ENGLISH MILES
0   100   200   300   400
Mountains thus

AFGHANISTAN

Kabul

BALUCHISTAN

R. Indus

R. Sutlej

THAR DESERT

Delhi

R. Jumna

HIMALAYAS

TIBET

R. Gogra

R. Ganges

R. Brahmaputra

R. Brahmaputra

BENGAL

Calcutta

VINDHYAS

R. Narbada

R. Tapti

R. Godavari

Bombay

WESTERN GHATS

Hyderabad

R. Kistna

ARABIAN

BAY OF

SEA

BENGAL

Madras

R. Cauvery

CEYLON

"GEOGRAPHIA" LTD

fatalism: a conditioning factor of all her peoples' development. Climate fundamentally affects a nation's history and character. The English climate, which as Charles II complained makes it possible on nearly every day of the year to take a five-mile walk, stimulates man to activity, whereas the Indian climate imposes a heavy mental and physical strain on its inhabitants and induces contemplation and even argument rather than action.

Two great river systems, the Indus and the Ganges, originate in the Himalayas and, fed the year round by everlasting snows, flow southwards, the Indus debouching into the Arabian Sea on the west, the Ganges turning east to the Bay of Bengal, there joining the Brahmaputra river which comes through Assam from Tibet. In the course of time silt, washed from the mountains, has built great alluvial plains across which these rivers now find their way, creating an extensive fertile area which supports two-thirds of India's present population.

Immediately to the south of the two-hundred-mile wide plains rise the east to west ridges of the Vindhya mountains, which virtually divide the country into Hindustan proper to the north and the Deccan to the south. Heavily wooded and rising in places to nearly five thousand feet the Vindhyas stand as an imposing but by no means impassable barrier, descending and giving way on the south to a plateau which, with an average height of over one thousand feet, forms the characteristic feature of the whole of South India. This plateau in general slopes—and most of its rivers run—from west to east, the western edge being sharply uptilted into a ridge of hills, the Western Ghats, which hinder quick and deep penetration of the country. By contrast on the other coast the wide Madras plain affords comparatively easy access.

In short, these bold climatic and geographic features have largely determined the pattern of India's life and history: clearly the bulk of her peoples have always lived in the northern plains, in Hindustan proper, and therein rests, as in the past and assuredly in the future, the heart of the country. Traversing and cultivating these level, fertile plains has always proved much easier and more profitable to man than penetrating and settling in the relatively arid uplands of the south.

At first glance at the map, India's natural defences both by sea and land seem formidable, but on closer investigation they prove to be more apparent than real. Wide oceans may separate her from other countries, but at certain seasons of the year men have never found difficulty in crossing these waters. Indeed, from the sea, except along her west coast, India lies open to the world. Moreover, the mountain rampart to the north is not impregnable. In the recent war against Japan we have seen that the north-eastern region, hitherto thought impassable to armies, may be pierced ; but it is from the north-west, through the most famous series of passes in the world, especially the Khyber from Afghanistan and Central Asia, that invaders throughout the course of India's history have worked their way into the fertile northern plains.

3. THE COMING OF THE ARYANS

India's history begins in the north-west. Sometime about 3000 B.C., that is, before the first pyramid of Egypt was built, there flourished in the Indus valley a highly civilized and widespread community. In 1924 at Harappa in the Punjab and at Mohenjo Daro in Sind, archaeologists uncovered a series of their cities—successively destroyed and rebuilt no less than seven times at Mohenjo Daro—the whole obviously representing a long period of development. Brick-built houses, and what even appear to be flats, each with its own wells and bathrooms, were found centring on stately palaces, temples and public baths, and all provided with an elaborate drainage system. The rich variety of household utensils, the painted pottery ware, the singular beauty of precious ornaments, the copper and bronze weapons of war, all illustrate the excellent quality of their crafts and culture. This civilization goes back in time to the period of the rise of the civilizations of Egypt, Assyria and Babylonia and, although all of them unquestionably came into contact, it cannot yet be determined whether their origins were quite separate, or whether this Indus valley culture had spread from Mesopotamia into India or *vice versa*.

Indeed, to say that we understand much of the ancient history of India would be wrong because we should be implying that a sufficiently large number of facts is known to the historian enabling him to create a reasonably coherent pattern or hypothesis of events. Actually over long stretches of years many of the relevant happenings are still unknown, and compared with the story of modern times, when the weight of information almost overwhelms the historian, this is a different kind of history; and all that we can properly do is to strike a bold outline.

We do not possess sufficient evidence, for example, to say whether the inhabitants of these Indus cities were the ancestors of the dark-skinned, flat-nosed peoples of whom we next have record living in these parts perhaps some 500 years later.

They are known to us as "dark-skinned Dasyus"—for thus they were described by their enemies, who were evidently light-skinned by comparison, and who pressed their way into India through the north-west passes from Central Asia, whence they had been driven possibly by the drying-up of their grazing grounds. For generation after generation these invading tribes—glorified by the Nazis in our own day under the name of Aryans but perhaps more properly to be described as Indo-Europeans—moved outwards from Central Asia, some into India, some towards Europe, some into Greece, where in that confined hothouse they created in an astonishingly short time one of the finest of human civilizations. Those of them who entered India have left a record of their achievements in their tribal hymns and songs, the Vedas, later written down and preserved as one of the oldest literatures in the world.

The contrast of colour between the invaders and the indigenous inhabitants struck deep, so deep that even to-day Indians set great store by fairness of skin. In a series of wars the dark-skinned peoples lost control of the fertile Indus valley. Geography determined their line of retreat; they could not move far to the south or south-east because of the Thar desert and the Vindhya mountains, and therefore they turned eastwards; some defended the watershed between the Indus and Ganges; and in the course of time were dislodged. Doubtless many were killed, many conquered and enslaved, the remnants of each new resistance probably making their way eastwards along the line of the Ganges until they could go no farther, or they took refuge in the foothills of the Himalayas and Vindhyas, or escaped through gaps in the mountains into South India.

4. THE GROWTH OF HINDUISM AND CASTE

These conquerors, at first nomads and in time settlers, who established themselves in the northern plains and later penetrated into South India, have done more to mould the life and civilization of India than any other people. In Sanskrit they brought with them a language new to India, which in its basic similarity to Latin, Greek, old Persian, Gothic and Celtic, suggests that these languages derive from a common Indo-European source—and in India, Sanskrit has given birth to a whole family of tongues, in particular, Hindi, Marathi, Bengali and Gujerati. In the contacts between the Aryans and the subject peoples the religion and society of Hinduism evolved and, subject to local and temporary interruptions, Hinduism controlled India politically until the thirteenth century A.D.; and when eventually political power passed to Muslim invaders, the Hindu rule of life continued to govern the conduct of the majority of the population; as it does the three hundred millions of Hindus to-day.

Hinduism constitutes not so much a religion in the European sense of creeds and worship, but rather a complete way of life. As its history shows, it is above all adaptable and absorptive of all manner of beliefs and precepts; never embodied in precise formulas, it comprehends on the one side the crudest animism, the worship of stones and trees, and on the other some of mankind's finest philosophic systems of thought. By Hindus a whole array of gods are popularly worshipped, each of them embodying different virtues and qualities of the Supreme Being—Brahma the Creator, Vishnu the Preserver, Siva the Destroyer, Nakshim the goddess of wealth, Rudra the god of rain, and many more—but just as important, and almost independently of the gods, the allied doctrines of rebirth and karma are accepted. The Hindu is said to be born and reborn on earth, his new form always depending on his previous behaviour until, with improvement, he achieves *nirvana*, eternal bliss, and becomes absorbed into the Supreme Being.

B

What the Hindu believes may not be capable of quick, easy definition, but what he must do in every detail of his daily life is clearly laid down for him and known by him. And we would not expect a religion and civilization which have been developing among a mixed and increasingly large population through a period of four thousand years to remain simple, or to be easily understood.

Of Hinduism, the caste system, which is at once the source of its strength and in the modern world its weakness, forms the dominant characteristic; and presents to outside view so complex a framework that one is apt to be appalled by the extent to which it fragments Indian society.

A caste is a social group, the membership of which is determined by birth; and within the fold of his caste the true Hindu must live and die. He cannot marry outside his caste, his choice of occupation is usually limited by the nature of his caste, what he may eat and drink and with whom is settled by the rules of his caste. For the individual, caste provides a social setting in which he finds a secure place, and in many ways, by stressing kinship and imposing a rigid social control, it protects him. Moreover, in a static civilization based on a parochial economy in which goods are produced for personal and local consumption rather than for widespread exchange, such a system makes for political and social stability; but through its fundamental unchangeability in a fast-changing world, and its divisions and essentially hierarchical nature in a world that is shrinking and becoming more homogeneous, it profoundly weakens Indian society as a whole.

To-day there exists a multitude of castes and sub-castes, well over three thousand in number, some deriving from tribal or racial elements, some occupational, being of the nature originally, perhaps, of guilds of artificers and craftsmen; some are territorial and some religious; origins so diverse in fact that it is unlikely that they could occur together more than once in place and time. Caste in its fullest sense, therefore, is an exclusively Indian phenomenon. In short, the caste system appears to have developed as a series of organic responses to the varied challenges of the situation. Originally the divisions appear to have been fewer and bolder; in particular there were the Brahmans or priestly groups; the Kshatriyas or royal and ruling warrior groups; the Vaishyas or trading and professional classes, and the Sudras or servile classes. We do not know exactly how or when these social classes began their process of unceasing sub-division and hardened into castes. Many writers have taken the view that Indian caste had a simple and single origin, but it seems more likely that such a complicated structure as the Indian caste system, with its almost unbelievable diversity of racial, religious and social customs, must have had a complex origin.

An early deep distinction undoubtedly occurred between the conquerors and the conquered, between the "dark-skinned dasyus" and the fair-skinned invaders, and in this respect it is significant that the Hindu word for caste is *varna*, which means colour. From among the downtrodden peoples will have come the groups to whom would be assigned the menial tasks of life; folk who, doing all the dirty work, would be pushed down the social scale, some no doubt more offensively unclean, who, for example, in a very hot climate where the pure preparation of food and drink is essential for health, would soon come to be feared as contaminators. In such groups it does not require too great an imaginative leap to see the origins of the present day untouchables, or depressed classes, of whom there are nearly fifty millions in India—pollutors of the caste Hindu's food, drink and even person, and consequently deemed outcaste; so to speak, recognized as part of the world of Hinduism only to be damned in this life.

Originally the ruling class—the Kshatriyas—stood undoubtedly superior to the Brahmans, and very likely tended to foster marriage within the group in order to maintain its superiority. An exclusionist marriage policy in one group would naturally tend to induce similar policies in other and inferior groups. As time passed, and the culture of the invaders inevitably fused with that of the indigenous peoples, the primitive structure of a society which had struck its tents and was on the march naturally gave way to the more complex organization of the settled community; particularly the simple nature worship revealed by the early Vedic hymns was transformed into a religion of complicated ceremonial and many gods. In these developments the function of the priest became all-important: he alone could perform the necessary elaborate ceremonies, he alone could faithfully interpret the wishes of the gods to man. When the ruling class could no longer safely get on without him, the social superiority of the Brahman was assured and he in his turn, to perpetuate his power, encouraged the habit of marriage within the class group. In the course of centuries —and we must not forget that we are speaking of one of the oldest civilizations in the world—habit was inevitably interpreted into dogma, and later, what was actually done was easily justified by elaborate theories.

The natural development of the Vaishyas and Sudras promoted the sub-division of Hindu society. Tribal organization and tribal quarrels undoubtedly favoured this process as did differences of occupation and the conventional acceptance of superior and inferior occupations. As in western Europe, skilled craftsmen and groups of families following the same craft came together; in India forming the nucleus of what were occupational castes in the making, one of their driving motives no doubt being the preservation of craft and trade secrets. Exclusionist marriage policies within a social group once applied in the higher castes, not only tended to force such a policy on the lower groups but also gave it a general social sanction.

Conquest and the colour bar may indeed have been important factors in the growth of caste but by themselves they clearly do not form the sole cause. Through the course of India's early history invaders continually passed from Central Asia into India—the Aryans, the Scythians, the Huns, the Muslims, to mention the more important—one and all forced by the configuration of the country to follow a similar path; and as these different and diverse groups perforce came to terms with each other, a society was built up into which any new unit could be fitted without difficulty, and in which any new sub-division within the community could easily be formed; a society absorptive and flexible.

These, then, form the main tendencies in early Hindu society: if one allows for the lapse of three thousand years in which they proliferate and work on one another in a country vast in area and among closely crowded peoples, whose

parochial agricultural economy throughout that time changed
hardly at all, one can begin to understand the existence and
strength to-day of the complex Hindu caste system.

5. THE HINDU POLITICAL LEGACY

It is important to recognize that India to-day is dominated
by this direct social inheritance from the remote past, so much so
that the political as distinct from the social legacy of ancient India
appears negligible by comparison. As we have seen the Aryan
invaders of India naturally enough first occupied the most fertile
land, that is to say the five rivers' area in the north-west, thence, as
the geography of the country dictated, turning eastwards along
the line of the Ganges. At first they established tribal settlements,
developing in the course of time into principalities and here
and there city states, and it seems that, like their kinsmen in
Greece, they brought with them local institutions and judicial
councils of a democratic type. But whereas in Greece the territorial compactness of the city state facilitated lively public
discussions of current problems and therefore promoted experiments in democracy, and its easily defensible boundaries
favoured the city's survival, the wide plains of north India gave
all the advantages to the vigorous military leader.

The political record of ancient India is therefore largely that
of a succession of similar military empires, some of them mighty
and splendid, but all of them dependent for their existence on
the personal vigour of the ruler and the strength of his army.
This factor indeed remains constant in the history of India down
to the time when the advent of speedy communications makes
possible both a coherent public life and the development of
free political institutions on a provincial or country-wide basis.

Few ruling families, in India or elsewhere, have succeeded in
producing a continuous stream of able and vigorous rulers, and
the life of these Indian empires, therefore, rarely extended
over more than three or four generations. Against this background it is understandable that such Hindu political writings
as have been preserved—particularly the outstanding
Arthasastra, "The Science of Polity," traditionally ascribed to
Kautilya, a famous minister of Chandragupta Maurya

(c. 300 B.C.)—are concerned not with the theory of the state but with giving practical advice on the creation and maintenance of an empire: and it is precisely the kind of advice which one would expect—the importance of ruthless efficiency in administration, how to overcome neighbouring states, how to divide and conquer one's enemies.

Equally suggestive was the traditional ceremony of horse sacrifice by which the aspiring emperor would justify his claim to his title. One of his horses with an armed escort was left free for a year to wander wheresoever it would: all the territories thus traversed were deemed part of the empire and opposition to the horse's passage was regarded as opposition to the emperor himself, until, at the year's end, the horse was led back to be sacrificed. Indeed, the extent of the plains encouraged universal dominion, and the idea of suzerainty over all the rulers of a large region, which formed the underlying assumption of the ceremony, became deeply rooted in Indian conceptions of government. To list in detail the histories of these empires would not be worth our while, but several of the most notable ruling families may be mentioned in illustration.

The first emperor worthy of the name of whom we have record is Chandragupta Maurya who in the fourth century B.C. extended his territories from Bengal to the Hindu Kush and possibly into Malwa and Gujarat. Under his successor the empire seems to have been consolidated and, under his grandson, Asoka, was pushed well into southern India. We are chiefly indebted for the facts of Asoka's life to his practice of having his edicts inscribed on rocks and pillars throughout his dominions, and consequently his is the first personality in Hindu history to stand out bold and clear. In many ways his rule was unique.

In a reign of some thirty-five years he began by pursuing the traditional policy of conquest, but after several successful campaigns, distressed by the misery of war, he turned to practising and teaching in his everyday administration the importance of the good life and of friendliness to others. In particular he sought to spread the religion of Buddhism, which had been growing in India since the sixth century B.C. He established many Buddhist shrines, laid particular stress on

"non-violence" and kindness to all living creatures, composed differences between Buddhist schools of thought and
despatched missionaries overseas. In Ceylon the faith took
firm hold and later also spread into Burma, Siam, Cambodia,
China and Japan where it still exercises considerable influence.
Soon after the death of Asoka the Mauryan empire broke up
and in the course of centuries in India the Buddhist religion,
for which he had cared most, gave way to and was absorbed by
Hinduism proper. But Asoka's magnificent conception of his
duties as a ruler and his demonstration of the power of goodness
when allied with intelligence still stand as a guide and
inspiration to Hindus to-day.

In the fourth and fifth centuries A.D. the Gupta empire,
comparable in size and stability with the Maurya, was created,
but meanwhile successive invasions of nomad Huns from
Central Asia had pushed into the plains from the north-west
and it was an irruption of allied tribes, the White Huns, that
finally smashed the Gupta empire itself. Few traces remain of
this whole series of invaders, for in time they were completely
absorbed into the vast extent of territory and the great number
of people, and, five centuries later, when the Turks followed the
path of the White Huns into India, Hindus only were found.

In short, the Hindu political legacy does not compare in
influence with its social heritage. Politically we are merely
left with an incompletely achieved dream of a united India
under an autocratic form of government, perpetuated in
traditions of a golden age. Hindu constructive genius clearly
took a social form. It mattered little that the governing power
was remote, weak and short-lived, when the Hindu's moral
duties and discipline could be locally and sharply enforced
by the village caste council of elders with public opinion and
the threat of outcasting as their weapons. Fundamentally the
Hindu caste assumption, that the way you must live and
behave among your equals is of greater import than the manner
in which you may be governed by a superior power, has far
wider human implications than any political doctrine.

Under such a system it was not the people's business to
defend the state, which in part explains both the relative ease
with which empire after empire was overthrown and the

frequent success of invaders from the north-west. The Muslims, who first reached India in the eighth century A.D., took advantage of this state of affairs and, differing from all previous invaders, not only conquered and settled but also to a great extent preserved their identity.

6. THE MUSLIM CONQUERORS

With the advent of the Muslims we come to another preponderating influence in the history of India. The extraordinary bursting out of Arab armies from Arabia, which followed on the preaching of Muhammad (569-632), belongs to the world's history: carrying with them the faith of Islam (an Arabic word meaning "resignation to the will of God") and offering the unbeliever the alternative of conversion or death, they passed through the strategic channel formed by Palestine and debouched into the Middle East and Central Asia. One wave reached Baluchistan in 650 and, sixty years later, under the Governor of Basra overflowed into Sind, which was then incorporated as a Muslim province under the Caliph of Baghdad. But Sind forms a backwater from which direct movement into India proper is barred by deserts, and nearly three centuries elapsed before the Muslim onslaught on India was resumed, and this time it came by the easier north-western approaches and in the persons not of Arabs but of Turks.

Towards the end of the tenth century a strong Turkish power established itself in Afghanistan and from its centre at Ghazni, eighty miles south of Kabul, delivered two terrible raids on north-west India and conquered the Punjab. In 1193 the state of Ghazni was supplanted by a new Turkish force, which, under Muhammad of Ghor, transferred its headquarters to Delhi in India and pursued a more serious policy of conversion and conquest. Henceforth Delhi, which guards the direct route from the north-west into the Gangetic plain, remained the strategic and political centre of Muslim India.

A short summary to complete the picture of Muslim political predominance in India will be helpful. During the thirteenth century the Turkish power, centred on Delhi, established sway over most of north India, and in the fourteenth century reached into the south. A confused period of struggle ensued extending through the fifteenth and into the sixteenth century, ending in the supremacy of Mughal invaders (also Turks and not Mongols) fresh from the north-west. By the seventeenth century their empire extended over almost the whole of India and it was its collapse in the following century which cleared the way for the political rise of the East India Company. The route and also the pattern of the Muslim conquest strikingly resembled that of the Indo-Europeans, and understandably so for the determining influence of geography remained constant.

Those Muslim forces, which had earlier pressed westwards along the North African coast and thence into Europe, ultimately met a combination of Christian powers and were repulsed; but in India no united Hindu front was presented. One by one the Hindu powers fought and one by one they were overcome.

The religion of Hinduism itself, however, determined the life of so many Indians over so wide an area, and the Muslims were so outnumbered, that one might have expected it, as with all previous alien influences, to absorb the faith of the newcomers. This did not happen; and a general notion of the areas where Islam succeeded in imposing itself permanently can be gained from the present position: in the north-west—that is Kashmir, the Frontier Province, Punjab and Sind together—Islam is the religion of more than three-quarters of the people: in the north-east more than half the population of Bengal are Muslims. In the rest of India Muslims form a small minority, usually less than one in ten.

7 . HINDUISM AND ISLAM

This astonishing ability of Islam in India in the midst of Hinduism to retain its identity and integrity demands explanation. The Muslims brought with them languages and laws new to India, namely Arabic, their sacred language, and their current tongue Persian, which in India gave birth to an even more popular language, Urdu; equally distinctive, their civil and religious laws obviously could apply only to Muslims and their criminal laws, which still further fortified their sense of separateness, pointed the moral of their political superiority by permitting a Muslim accused of crime to be convicted only on the evidence of Muslims. Moreover, the Muslims inside India were continually reinforced and sustained from without: the centre of the Muslim world lay beyond India and whether for political motives, such as the confirmation of conquests, or for religious reasons, such as the essential pilgrimage to Mecca, Muslim attention was steadily drawn outside India. This foreign influence, strengthened by an antagonism inevitable between new conquerors and their subject peoples, offset the absorbent power of Hinduism. Most fundamental of all, it would have been difficult to find a religion that contrasted more sharply with Hinduism than Islam.

The Hindu accepts many gods; the Muslim maintains, "There is no God but God, and Muhammad is the apostle of God." In the Koran—the sacred book revealed to mankind through Muhammad—the Muslim finds codified his creed and proper pattern of life: the Hindu relies on no such comparable formula. The Muslim believes in a final day of judgment, the Hindu accepts the doctrine of rebirth. Islam is a brotherhood, all Muslims being held to be equal before God; Hinduism, on the other hand, is founded on inequality and is essentially hierarchical. Islam is little concerned with ritual, its members directly approach God; Hinduism is luxuriant in ceremony in which the priest plays an essential part. At all points Islam—simple, clear-cut, assertive—stands opposed to Hinduism—elaborate, roughly defined, absorptive—and their adherents could find few means of making contact: they could not eat together, they could not intermarry, and they quickly grew to despise each other's cultures, which indeed were mutually meaningless.

8. MUSLIM POLICIES

In their treatment of the Hindus three broad policies lay open to the Muslim conquerors: first, to offer the orthodox choice of conversion to Islam or death or slavery; secondly, to tolerate Hinduism whilst establishing forever the Hindu as an inferior being and making him pay physically or financially, as the whim of the moment decided, for his obstinacy; thirdly, and by far the most far-sighted and difficult, to work to achieve a genuinely homogeneous Indian society. During the whole period of Muslim political dominance, from the thirteenth to the eighteenth century, none of these policies was consistently pursued. The first, indeed, was never seriously tried. Precepts laid down in Mecca had been modified long before the Muslim wave reached India, and once the initial dash was over it became customary to allow the Hindu population to remain undisturbed, subject to the payment of *jizya*, a poll-tax, and of *kharaj*, land revenue, representing a share of the annual produce of the cultivated land.

In short, over most of the country the peasant sowed and reaped as before but paid his revenue to a Muslim instead of to a Hindu ruler. The cleavage in social and religious matters remained complete and therefore the second policy, that of "contemptuous toleration," came to be accepted and, carried out over a period of centuries, it inflicted a deep humiliation on the Hindus. Various Muslim rulers toyed with the third policy, that of trying to create a truly homogeneous Indian society, but only one, Akbar (1556–1605), showed sufficient foresight and held power long enough to put his theories to the test. In him we can see a true vision of greatness.

Grandson of Babur, the first of the great Mughal emperors, Akbar inherited at the age of thirteen a precarious kingdom in the Punjab but, fiercely ambitious, possessed of a lively and determined mind, with the capacity to see quickly to the heart of a problem and take instant decisions, he sought throughout his life to bring all India under one central authority, and by the time of his death, at the age of sixty-two, he had almost succeeded. Moreover, perceiving that political without social unity would not long endure, and with a personal inclination to resolve his own intellectual doubts, he tried to create a religion which would bring Hindus and Muslims together and perhaps combine the best of all faiths. He was the first great Indian of modern times to rise to the conception of governing the country on behalf of all its peoples alike. In 1582 he proclaimed the new religion, "The Divine Faith," constituting himself the sole authoritative exponent. He regarded Muslim orthodoxy with disfavour. To cut off Indian Muslims from foreign influences he required them to recognize him as Caliph and to forgo the pilgrimage to Mecca. Local Muslim risings were easily quelled and the Muslim leaders dispossessed of their lands, a policy which Akbar generally applied to rebellious Muslims. His attitude towards Hindus and Hindu rulers contrasted strongly: on defeat they were usually given an honoured and assured position within the empire; and the taxes on Hindus and Muslims were equalized. He himself sought and gained the support of the leading Hindu Rajput chiefs, did not hesitate to marry Rajput princesses, and often entrusted Hindu generals with the command of his armies.

This design of redressing the balance of past policy in favour of the Hindus, and at the same time isolating Indian Muslims from Islam, might have succeeded in its ultimate object, the fusing of the two cultures, had it been systematically applied over a very long period of time: as it was, Akbar's composite religion disappeared with his death, and his successors soon returned to the simpler, more lucrative policy of putting the interests of Islam and the Muslim ruling class first.

Indeed, Aurangzeb (1658–1707), the last of the great Mughals, went so far in this direction, persecuting and heavily taxing the Hindus on every possible occasion, that it seemed that the empire was organized for the benefit of Muslims alone.

Sporadic Hindu risings took place in the north, the Rajput chiefs withdrew their valuable military support, and in the Deccan, immediately to the east and south-east of Bombay, in an area consisting of a narrow coastal plain and mountainous hinterland full of flat-topped hills, a new Hindu power, that of the Marathas, was emboldened to defy the empire. Living in an agriculturally poor area the Marathas had long eked out a frugal, hard existence by raiding and fighting as mercenaries. When attacked they retired into the perfect guerrilla country of their homeland. Their light cavalry became one of the best military weapons in India, and under the inspiring, bold leadership of Sivaji (1627–1680) who did not hesitate to challenge the empire, they struck repeatedly and successfully at the Mughal north-south lines of communication, until the Maratha power threatened to dominate the whole of central India. It might have been expected that the deep, country wide challenge of the Muslims would provoke an overwhelming Hindu nationalist response, but the means of making such a widespread, effective response, particularly the absence of quick communications, were lacking and the divisions among the Hindus themselves, reinforced by the frustrating Maratha policy of levying toll on Hindu and Muslim alike, curbed the growth of their political power.

Meanwhile Aurangzeb, just as ambitious as Akbar yet lacking his military and political skill, had been exhausting the empire by simultaneously waging a defensive war in the vital north-west approaches and striving to push his territories still further towards the southern tip of India and into Assam in the north-east. When he died in 1707 the empire finally fell apart. The central administration disintegrated under the stress of a prolonged struggle for the succession between his sons, of the continued attacks of the Marathas in the south, and of an invasion in 1738-9 of northern India through the north-west passes, during which the Persian King, Nadir Shah, sacked Delhi, the capital city, and slaughtered its inhabitants.

The Mughal empire differed in degree rather than in kind from its Hindu predecessors. Its foreign policy—the indefinite extension of its conquests—had been similar, and like them it had been unable either to guarantee India against invasion in the north-west or long to safeguard its lines of communication south of the Vindhyas. Like them, too, the government of the state was necessarily military and autocratic, and therefore the care of the army and the protection of the person of the ruler, usually by an organization of spies, formed its first concern.

8. THE ECONOMIC ASPECT

Taking a broad survey of the history of Hindu and Muslim India we can see that the country was too large, its population too numerous, for even a majority of its peoples to be seriously disturbed at any one time by invasions, wars or political upsets. Drought and famine—the stock topics of both Hindu and Muslim story-tellers—alone did that, otherwise the social and economic life of the people flowed steadily in its accustomed channels. The great bulk of the income of the country was provided by the peasants working on the land and raising crops which are still the main staples of the country—rice, wheat, barley, millets and pulses, oilseeds and sugar cane—and it was the needs of this local, small-scale agriculture on a consumption rather than an exchange basis that determined the life of most Hindus and Muslims alike. On this basis Indian economy remained parochial, primitive and essentially static, and the culture of the countryside and the court, often brilliant in the extreme under the Mughals, widely diverse.

Necessarily both Hindu and Muslim rulers drew their financial strength from their cultivators and took it in the most convenient form of land revenue, traditionally forming one-sixth of the crop, though on occasion it may even have been one-third or one-half. The broad system of revenue administration was not radically altered under Muslim rule, although under Akbar, in fairness, comprehensiveness and efficiency, it became more scientific and far surpassed anything that had gone before.

The production of cotton cloth and goods early became important in India, and soon took a dominant place in the whole commercial situation, for as sea-routes were opened up the peoples of South-East Asia and the Malayan Archipelago eagerly sought Indian cottons. In bulk the sea-borne trade was not great, in Akbar's time, for instance, certainly not exceeding 60,000 tons a year, and no large scale organizations for the management of money or trade seem to have developed and little use was made of economic means for political ends; but along the trade routes Indian cultures, whether Hindu, Buddhist or Muslim, spread until they made contact with China on the east, south-east and north-east. Commercially and culturally, in Hindu and Muslim times, India became influential in those areas over which in the recent war against Japan her armies have had to exercise a strategic control. In effect her early civilizations marked out India's proper spheres of influence and interest.

9. THE CLEAVAGE OF INDIA

The majority of Hindu and Muslim rulers practised the art of administration and diplomacy quite divorced from ethical considerations. Unlimited conquest was their motive, but whereas the Hindu empires bequeathed to Indians vague aspirations of a united India, the Mughal empire, once Akbar's policy had clearly failed, emphasized the deep cleavage in society that the coming of Islam had created. In our own day, with the Indian National Congress, which is predominantly Hindu, demanding a united India, and the Muslim League striving successfully to divide India, we can see the extent to which the remote past directly influences current Indian events. The broad effect of Islam on Hinduism was to make it more stubbornly aware of itself, and no splendour of political unity or central administrative efficiency could disguise the fact that fundamentally India had been broken in two.

CHAPTER II

THE RISE OF THE EAST INDIA COMPANY

I. THE PORTUGUESE IN THE EAST

A QUARTER century before the Mughals began to conquer northern India the first Portuguese fleet under Vasco da Gama anchored off the Malabar coast; and whilst the Mughals went on to conquer the Indian mainland the Portuguese made themselves lords not only of Indian waters, but of all the eastern seas.

Vasco da Gama's justly famous voyage to India in 1498 was not a merely personal or incidental success but the culmination of a painstaking and brilliant scientific achievement. It represented the combined creation through experiment by many men of a dependable ocean-going vessel so equipped as to be guided surely and safely round the world. The Portuguese were favourably situated for bold seafaring. Unable, like the Spanish and the Arabs, to command land-locked and relatively sheltered waters such as the Mediterranean, they were forced to sail the oceans and, in Portugal itself, their schools of navigation consolidated practice with theory. Thus through the fifteenth century they slowly pushed their seaway and their trade down the west African coast and round the Cape of Good Hope.

Where they led it was fairly easy for others to follow, and, during the sixteenth and seventeenth centuries, their European rivals, the Dutch, the English and the French, all trained in the same hard Atlantic school, sent fleets to the Orient; and in India in particular the interaction of these representatives of a dynamic European civilization created forces which in the course of time have destroyed India's static civilization.

India's geographic and climatic conditions favoured a static civilization. Indian seafaring, for example, had developed early and quickly, and large mercantile fleets had come into existence,

INDIA
TO ILLUSTRATE
THE RISE OF THE E. I. Co.
ENGLISH MILES
0   100   200   300   400

for it was comparatively easy to sail to the Middle East or to South-East Asia if one sailed at the right time of year. There was a time to sail and a time to shelter in port, and experiment by sailing out of season was precluded by the strength and persistence of the regular monsoon winds and storms. Whereas in the Atlantic the elements could usually be overcome, in the Indian Ocean they tended, when adverse, to be overwhelming. It is not surprising, therefore, that European nations should have developed sea-power whilst the rulers of the virtually self-sufficient Indian mainland remained content with seaways.

Similarly in agriculture, early development in India was easy and swift. The rains, on which all growth depended, usually came yearly at the same time, and a mere scratching of the surface and sowing of seed was sufficient to yield a rich harvest. But if the rains failed in any one region, as often happened, the result there was certain famine and death. Indian conditions were such, therefore, as to discourage experimental farming, experimental seafaring, and, more generally, in practical matters an experimental frame of mind, and we can understand why it was that in the sixteenth and seventeenth centuries, when Europe was learning how to navigate the oceans, how to apply seapower, how to wield artillery, how to organize representative government, how to cultivate religious toleration, how to use money in promoting trade, India politically, socially and economically seems by comparison to have been at a standstill. We can also understand that in an armed clash between the two civilizations Europe would at first prevail.

The Portuguese motives in voyaging to the East, as in most long-planned and developing ventures, were mixed, but predominant were the desires to profit through trade, to spread Christianity and to combat Islam. In the eighth century Muslim armies had overrun all Spain including Portugal, and although soon beaten back they continued to harass Europe across the Mediterranean. In the fifteenth century the Portuguese fought bitterly against their forces in North-West Africa and it was natural to continue the struggle in the East, the more so because the Portuguese passage of the Cape in effect outflanked and broke the Arab monopoly of the land trade routes between

East and West. The Portuguese particularly sought spices. Europe's diet compared with to-day was monotonous: more important, its winter meat taken without spices was quite unpalatable. The cattle, for want of winter foodstuffs, were usually slaughtered in the autumn and the meat, which was dried or pickled, assumed so distinct a flavour that only spices sufficed to disguise it. Moreover, in the somewhat noisome society of the time, spices provided a desirable fragrance; and Cardinal Wolsey's pomander, for example, stuffed with cloves, was not carried by him at Henry VIII's court as a mere ornament.

Few in numbers, the Portuguese were not concerned with extensive land conquests, but, conscious of the fragility of their extended communications round the Cape, they were determined to seek an immediate and decisive victory at sea, followed by a quick turnover in trade; and fortune was with them, for they found themselves on the Malabar coast favourably placed right in the centre of a valuable three-cornered trade.

Cotton goods had long regularly passed from India to the Malay Archipelago in exchange for spices, silks, and drugs, which in turn were transferred into Arab ships in the ports of South India, along with the pepper from the hinterland. The whole trade from South India to the Near East had thus fallen into Arab hands and in the past they had not hesitated to exploit their monopoly. The Portuguese, therefore, on the one side received a warm welcome from the long-suffering South Indian producers and, on the other, a direct challenge from the Arab exporters.

The outcome of the ensuing struggle clearly rested on the test of sea-power, and the Portuguese, under the brilliant direction of Albuquerque, their first Governor in the East (1509–1515), not only defeated the Arab fleet in close combat but also devised a sea strategy which gave them control of the trade routes of the Indian Ocean as a whole. The plan itself was simple, but that Albuquerque, with scanty information and in so short a time, was able so quickly and successfully to apply it, bears clear testimony to his genius as a commander and particularly to his powers of seeing straight to the heart of a problem and of taking quick decisions. Albuquerque argued that there were three essentials in controlling the trade, first to establish a strong central base, secondly to deny easy entry to the Indian Ocean to other sea-powers by building fortresses to guard the narrow waters, and thirdly to maintain a constant patrol of the main routes. Substantially he was able to carry the plan into effect. In the confused Indian political situation the seaport of Goa was seized without difficulty in 1510 to form the Portuguese headquarters; in the east Malacca was captured and fortified to control the Straits, on the west Ormuz similarly to dominate the Persian Gulf.

The attacks on Aden, the fall of which would have completed the project, failed, but the capture later of Diu enabled the Portuguese to regulate the flow of shipping to the Red Sea. By these means the Arab traders were driven from Indian waters, leaving the Portuguese supreme, a position which they maintained throughout the sixteenth century.

Wherever the Portuguese settled their influence went deep, for in religious matters they were as fanatical as the Muslims; and to this the existence of Roman Catholic populations at Goa and other Indian cities to-day bears testimony. But their expansion was finally limited by the strength of Portugal in Europe. A home population of scarcely two millions could hardly support vast empires both in the New World and in the East, and it was inevitable that preference should be given to its South American territories whence was drawn the supply of precious metals which financed its home and Eastern trade. In fact it does not appear that the Portuguese greatly expanded the trade of the Eastern seas but without question they made it safer and more regular.

2. THE DUTCH AND ENGLISH EAST INDIA COMPANIES

The fate of the Portuguese power in the East largely depended on developments in Europe. There during the course of the sixteenth century the Dutch gradually revealed the growing weakness of Portugal by monopolizing the European distribution of Eastern produce which in the first place they bought in the markets of Portugal itself. In 1580 Philip II of

Spain overran Portugal and, in eclipsing her power, challenged the Dutch by excluding them from Portuguese ports. The Dutch were forced, therefore, to look to the East itself for their customary supplies of pepper, cloves and cinnamon.

They did not hesitate to make the attempt to supplant their bitterly hated national enemies in the East, and groups of merchants quickly fitted out small expeditions which from 1596 made successive voyages to Java and Sumatra. They finally joined forces in 1602, with the full backing of the state, to form a powerful and wealthy Dutch East India Company. Simultaneously in England several hundred merchants of London, who had played a great part in meeting the challenge of Spanish sea-power, had been seeking Crown approval for an Eastern trading venture and, on 31 December 1600, Queen Elizabeth granted them a charter as the English East India Company.

The Dutch reached the East before the English and in much greater strength. They had gone for spices, and therefore made directly for the East Indies, the centre of the spice trade, and with their superior naval technique, ships and weapons quickly crippled Portuguese power in that area and themselves set up their headquarters at Batavia in Java. When the English arrived Dutch power in the Archipelago was already too firmly established to be displaced and, after a prolonged and vain attempt to cling to Bantam in Java, during which the Dutch made it quite clear that they were determined to exclude all other powers from their chosen stronghold, the English turned to the mainland of India, albeit in their view a second-best, less desirable area for trade.

From the beginning the policies of the two Companies diverged. The Dutch clearly sought to displace the Portuguese and assume the monopoly of the spice trade: the English had neither the strength nor the will to do this and therefore took second place, and generally looked round for trade where they could find it. Had England not held her own in European waters her Eastern venture would have failed altogether.

Through the seventeenth century the Dutch steadily established their dominion over Indian waters: in 1641 Malacca fell to them, in 1656 Colombo in Ceylon, in 1663 Cochin, leaving the Portuguese in India with Goa only. India gained by the Dutch and English supersession of the Portuguese, for the latter had shown themselves cruelly intolerant whilst both the former had at least learnt the merit of religious toleration. In general policy, too, they differed, for whereas the Portuguese found it sufficient for their purpose to control sea-routes, the Dutch, facing greater competition and disposing of the necessary strength in numbers and material, began to establish control over the production areas themselves, completely achieving their object in the Archipelago and partially succeeding in South India and Ceylon. They therefore became both a military and naval power, able to protect their territory but certainly not strong enough to compete in any way on the mainland of India with the growing land power of the Mughal empire.

Indeed, for the Dutch, as at first for the English, India was of secondary interest. The greatest trade demand in the Archipelago, as both Dutch and English soon discovered, was for Indian cotton goods and they therefore voyaged to India to meet this need, but once there both companies found that they were welcomed as bringing the most desired kind of trade, namely hard cash in the form of silver and gold and also luxury goods to exchange for India's calicoes, indigo, yarn, saltpetre and sugar. This voyage to India, therefore, soon became an essential part of the Dutch trade circle, affording as their export of luxuries increased an invaluable relief from the need to carry from Europe large quantities of precious metals. The trade itself was insufficient in volume to affect the economic life of India as a whole, and among Indians it was the middleman in the coastal towns rather than the peasant who benefited.

The Mughal court was not above using some of the luxury articles which were brought from Europe, such as mirrors, chandeliers and greyhounds, but in so far as it deigned to notice the activities of the Dutch and English merchants on the fringe of its empire, it was disposed to condone rather than discourage. The disadvantages of finding the monopoly of Indian sea-power in the hands of one nation, the Portuguese, had been only too clear, and the policy of approving of more than one European company, each of which might at need be played off against the others, was much to be preferred. English settlements were therefore sanctioned at Madras and Masulipatam in the south, and on the west coast at Surat, and Dutch centres also at the two latter places and at Pulicat, twenty miles north of Madras: and in the 1680's both powers were also allowed to settle in Bengal.

These rented settlements or factories, as they were termed, at which goods could be stored or quickly exchanged, were essential in a circular and lengthy sea-borne trade, and the value of the stores that accumulated soon led the Companies to seek permission to build fortifications. The Dutch were thus able to protect Pulicat; and the English erected Fort St. George to cover Madras, and in 1668 the gift to the Company by Charles II of the island of Bombay, which had come to him as part of the dowry of his wife, Catherine of Braganza, enabled them to establish a new and safer headquarters on the west coast.

This problem of defending the factories grew more urgent during the reign of Aurangzeb (1658–1707), for, although the Mughal territories continued to grow in extent, the grip of Delhi over the provinces was clearly failing. In these circumstances both Dutch and English attempted to assert some degree of independence of the local rulers and in turn suffered increasing exactions, especially in Bengal. In London the Company's governors thought that their Bengal trade needed the protection of a fort similar to Bombay and Madras—they wanted to found, in the words of their spokesman, Sir Josia Child, "a large well-grounded sure English dominion in India"—and they ordered their agent, Job Charnock, to seize Chittagong as a suitable headquarters.

This was tantamount to declaring war on the Mughal Empire, and such an action, so near to the northern centres of Muslim power, could not be ignored. Also, unfortunately for the English, the strength of Aurangzeb's forces had been completely under-estimated. The attack on Chittagong failed, six of the Company's factories were lost, Bombay was besieged, and the English were forced to sue for peace. The terms granted were generous, for on payment of a fine the English under Charnock were allowed to settle at Calcutta and build Fort William, and shortly afterwards, to assist them in bearing the expense of this fort, they were permitted to rent three neighbouring villages.

It will be noted that, subject to the same physical and political circumstances, the early development of all the Companies in India conformed to a similar pattern: first the long voyage followed by the creation of the factory, then the protection of the latter by a fort paid for, in part at least, out of the revenues of adjoining territory, which was rented from the local Indian ruler.

The English, as it happened, had fortified their three main centres only just in time, for, after the death of Aurangzeb in 1707, the Mughal Empire fell to pieces. The defences of the north-west collapsed before Nadir Shah of Persia who sacked Delhi in 1739, an exploit repeated in 1754 by the forces of the Durani family who had meanwhile conquered the Punjab. In the provinces the Mughal viceroys set themselves up as independent monarchs; the Nizam in Hyderabad, and other Muslims as Nawabs in Oudh, Bengal, Bihar and the Carnatic, and self-made Hindu rulers established themselves in Mysore and Travancore in the south. The Marathas, a stronger power altogether, mastered Central India and for a time the dominion of all India lay within their reach. But, although controlling extensive and productive areas, they still continued their early policy of long-ranging, pillaging raids on their neighbours.

Hindus and Muslims, their villages and towns held to ransom or plundered, their lives freely taken, suffered alike. Evidently Hinduism was still too vague a political force for the Marathas to realize the possibilities of an India-wide Hindu nation state, and when, in 1761, their largest, and incidentally most ill-managed and cumbrous army, was decisively beaten by the forces of the Duranis at Panipat near Delhi, they lost their opportunity. Politically and economically India began to dissolve in chaos.

Clearly the period was one of great misery for the mass of the people, but for the English in their fortified centres at Madras, Bombay and Calcutta it was one of growing prosperity and strength. All three were cities of refuge, havens of quiet, regular government in the midst of disorder, where all comers could be sure of religious toleration and a not too partial administration of justice. As Aungier, Governor of Bombay, declared to his assistants, "Formerly the name of the English nation was known in these parts only by the honesty of their traffic, but now, I trust in God, through the just execution of their laws. . . . The inhabitants of this island consist of several nations and religions, but you, when you sit in this seat of judgment, must look upon them with one single eye as I do, without distinction of nation or religion." Under these guiding policies the Indian population of Calcutta alone between 1700 and 1750 rose from 15,000 to 100,000, and Bombay and Madras likewise expanded. Their wealth was largely Indian, for all the great Indian trading and banking houses set up agencies there, but the English Company's trade through the three towns also grew and in the same period more than doubled itself: certainly, a trade valuable enough in English eyes to be worth defending and fighting for.

This position of affairs could not last indefinitely, for areas of order and disorder, of expanding trade and economic misery were too closely juxtaposed. If the trade of the Company's settlements and the happiness of its inhabitants were to continue to grow—and this was desirable—some attempt sooner or later would have had to be made to restore order, and with it the possibility of peaceful development, in the neighbouring territories. Had such a decision offered itself and been refused, it would have been monstrous. As it happened, however, the constant rivalry of the European Companies, placed in a setting of Indian political and economic decline, made the taking of such a decision inevitable. The only questions remaining were who would make the first move and how soon.

In European waters the Dutch were slowly yielding their naval pre-eminence, which was reflected in the East in their steady retirement into the Eastern Archipelago; and it was in fact the French Company, the latest European power to arrive in Indian waters, which acted first.

3. THE FRENCH-ENGLISH CLASH

The French Company had reached India in 1664, settling on both the Malabar and Coromandel coasts and establishing a strong point at Pondicherry, about a hundred miles to the south of Madras; but for many years it counted for little. Unlike the Dutch and English Companies it was the product, not of a spontaneous urge to trade in Eastern produce, but of the deliberate state policy of the French Government, and its function and strength therefore almost entirely depended upon the ebb and flow of politics in Paris. Understandably, its most active agents were more concerned with politics than trade, and more than one of them mooted the advantages that would be gained from intervening on one side or the other in the unending struggles between Indian states.

In these circumstances the clash of national ambitions in Europe finally determined the broad policies, successes and failures of the European Companies in India, and in the War of Austrian Succession, which broke out in 1744, France and England took opposing sides. The conflict was fought out on land and sea and inevitably spread to the East, where it caught both French and English Companies ill-prepared for fighting, but the former with a newly appointed and extraordinarily able Governor, Joseph Dupleix. Ambitious and prescient, strong-willed and resourceful, with over twenty years' experience of Indian conditions, Dupleix saw that the break-up of the Mughal Empire had created the French opportunity of becoming an Indian power just at the time when his home government was willing to provide sufficient forces in ships and soldiers to deal with the English in southern India. But the English stubbornly resisted: indeed, their small naval squadron captured the French China fleet, but the lack of a suitable sea base finally wore down their strength. The French, on the other hand, enjoyed the inestimable advantage of a good base at Mauritius, which although over 2,000 miles away was yet equal to their needs.

In the absence of the English fleet the French besieged Madras by sea and land. The English invoked the aid of the local Indian ruler, the Nawab of Arcot, who sent to their help two large armies consisting of cavalry according to the established Indian practice: but each in succession was met and swept away like flies by the concentrated fire-power of small French forces of trained musketeers and field artillery. These victories were all the more notable because the French, as had been their practice for some years past, used as an integral part of their army several companies of sepoys, a name applied to Indian infantry trained by Europeans.

Despite all efforts Madras remained in French hands until the general European peace of 1748 stipulated its return. For both Companies, therefore, the war appeared inconclusive, but in fact its lessons were of the greatest significance. It was evident that small forces—for neither side had disposed of more than 2,000 Europeans—trained and disciplined on the western model and using the new system of tactics and fire-power could destroy large Indian armies. The way to the domination of India stood clear, and there was no good reason why the European Companies should not interfere in Indian politics: indeed, by so doing they might in a land of chaos even spread and maintain law and order. Lastly, by implication, whichever European sea-power could control the sea route to India could also dominate India itself, and during the succeeding sixty years France and Britain fought out this issue.

The peace of 1748 left both the French and English Companies not only financially impoverished but with more troops than they needed, and Dupleix characteristically at once set about solving his problems in one grand scheme, each part of which would set off the rest. He felt that by supporting claimants to the thrones of the South Indian states of Hyderabad and the Carnatic he could both usefully employ and support his troops and at the same time ensure a sufficiently large French dominion to yield financial surpluses which might then be exported to France in the form of goods. He did not inform the Paris authorities of his intentions but, arguing to himself that his plan would obviate the need for the always unpopular remission of silver from France, relied rather on the delayed but cogent appeal of a profitable *fait accompli.*

In Hyderabad all went well and from 1750 to 1755 his representative, Charles de Bussy, in effect ruled the state, but in the Carnatic the French were checkmated, for there the English in Madras felt the threat closely, and—refusing to yield their position and trade—took the obvious alternative of supporting the Nawab whom Dupleix sought to displace. In the struggle that followed the English Company threw up a military genius in Robert Clive, who at the crisis of attack held on for fifty glorious days to the strategic centre of Arcot, and thereby blocked the French designs. In 1754 the Paris authorities, who did not appreciate the significance of what was happening in India, suddenly lost confidence in Dupleix and recalled him, at the same time making a truce with the English. In London clearer views prevailed, for the Company's directors had come to the conclusion that if they did not increase their sea power they would lose their factories and their trade. New ships were built and a squadron was borrowed from the Navy with the result that, in the Seven Years' War which broke out in 1756, the English drove the French fleet to refuge at Mauritius and easily captured the French stronghold of Pondicherry.

Thus far Calcutta in Bengal had remained relatively undisturbed, but in the same year the young and newly-elected Nawab of Bengal, Siraj-ud-daula, foreseeing that it was only a matter of time before the European policies in South India were also applied in Bengal, decided to strike first. In the India of that generation, when might was right, the policy of strike first and talk afterwards was both accepted and profitable. Fort William, almost undefended, soon fell and the Company's servants at Calcutta either suffered imprisonment or fled, but again the English control of the sea proved conclusive. A relief expedition from Madras under Clive reached Calcutta by sea, easily recaptured Fort William, and, after forcing the Nawab to make peace, went on to capture the French settlement of Chandernagore.

Shortly afterwards, when rival Bengal factions showed signs of uniting to exclude Siraj-ud-daula, Clive did not hesitate to join them, and with a force of no more than 3,000 marched against the Nawab and his unwieldy army and, displaying the brilliance of his own incisive mind and the superiority of European military technique, completely beat him at Plassey (1757). Clive then established his own nominee, Mir Jafar, as Nawab and did not hesitate to announce, what was true in fact, that the English were masters of Bengal. Clive was undoubtedly a great man of action—ever on the "go" perhaps because he had such a prodigious capacity for boredom—but, as he admitted, his task had proved easy. Let it be granted that his methods were not always honourable, that bribery, chicanery, even forgery played their part, and that he and his officers made suspiciously large fortunes, yet even so Clive's standards were immeasurably higher than the Indian practice of the day; and one cannot but admire the resolution and decision of his character.

By 1763, when the world-wide Seven Years' War came to an end, the British, profiting by the Portuguese and Dutch experiments in using sea-power and by the French discovery of the superiority of European land forces, were firmly established in Bengal through Calcutta and in the Carnatic through Madras. Moreover, they had also apparently solved the problem—which had always baffled and finally broken the strength of the Hindu and Muslim empires—of maintaining themselves on both sides of the Vindhya mountains. Through their use of sea power they were in effect outflanking the difficulty; and if more decisions were to be taken or forced on them to expand farther there was no question that the Ganges valley with its easy and secure water communications and fertile provinces offered the more attractive military and economic possibilities. In short, the British summed up the naval and military experience of all the European Companies in the East, and used it in Bengal, that is, in the area which led directly to the heart and wealth of India.

The Company's grip on Bengal was soon tested, for in 1764 the Nawab, Mir Kasim, successor of Mir Jafar, attempted to reassert his authority by joining forces with his neighbours, the ruler of Oudh and Shah Alam, the titular Mughal emperor; but they were all heavily defeated at Buxar. In the following year Clive clarified the Company's position by accepting from the emperor the right to administer the revenues of Bengal and Bihar and at the same time, with the idea of creating buffer states to safeguard Bengal, made treaties of alliance with him and with Oudh. The more straightforward decision of at once asserting British sovereignty over Bengal might have been taken but the Company's home authorities and Clive himself foresaw in this course endless difficulties with Parliament and with France and Holland, and preferred the evil of retaining in Bengal a puppet Indian Nawab and divided responsibilities.

Clive left India in 1767 and his great successor, Warren
Hastings—created in 1773 Governor-General of all the
Company's territories—inherited the task of justifying the
East India Company's right to exist as one of the major Indian
powers. His aims were two-fold: on the one hand to create an
administrative system for the areas in which the Company
wielded power, which we shall discuss in the next chapter, on
the other hand to maintain these territories against attack—
which seemed certain to come—from the French once more
and also from the Indian powers, each jealous of the other and
all jealous of the Company. The most threatening by far were
Mysore in the south, recently consolidated into a fighting state
under a bold adventurer, Haidar Ali; secondly the Marathas,
about to renew their attempt to conquer northern India; and
thirdly, lying uneasily between them, the forces of Hyderabad.

So long as these powers quarrelled among themselves
and the scattered English Presidencies of Bengal, Madras and
Bombay maintained a united front based on control of the
sea, all went well for Hastings; but in 1779–80 Britain found
herself in a grim situation, the like of which she was not again
to experience until 1940–41.

Her war with the American colonies (1776–83) was hopelessly mismanaged on land and sea and the combination of
French and Spanish power cost her the command of American
waters: simultaneously in the East the French fleet under
Suffren, one of the greatest of French admirals, neutralized
English sea-strength and French diplomacy at last succeeded in
inducing Haidar Ali, Hyderabad and the Marathas to join
against the English. On top of this, the three Presidencies dis-
agreed completely about the extent of Hastings' superintending
powers, and in Bengal he himself was fretted to the point of
desperation by the fantastic opposition of part of his own
council incited by the notorious Philip Francis. But by the
skin of his teeth, and without always pausing to question the
rightness of his acts, he held on: whenever he could, he made
war terrible to his enemies, until, as he knew would happen,
they once more fell to quarrelling among themselves. Only a
man of the greatest strength of character, of outstanding
ability, of resolute faith in Britain and himself could have

held on so long: and in 1785, on returning home, he left the Company in India hardly more extensive than when he had taken charge but welded at last into an Indian power with a coherent policy. In this position, without betraying Indians and British alike, it was impossible for the Company to retire or to stand still, and in fact Warren Hastings, without realizing it, had made possible the British empire *of* India.

On their return to England both Clive and Hastings were called to account for their rule in India, and in the process, although each in turn was finally acquitted, the British Parliament made it quite clear that the Company's rule in India would have to conform more closely to English standards and, as a first move in this direction, Pitt's India Acts of 1784 and 1786 were passed. Pitt said his plan was, "to give to the Crown the power of guiding the politics of India with as little means of corrupt influence as possible," and he laid down that henceforward the Company's directors and policy were to be supervised by a Board of Control, the President and only effective member of which was to hold a seat in the British ministry of the day. Through him the cabinet came to exert the decisive influence in the appointment of the governor-general, who tended henceforth to be chosen from English political life.

Never again was the governor-general to be placed in Hastings' impossible situation: his authority over Madras and Bombay was therefore plainly declared, and also the right to overrule his Council and even to assume on occasion the duties of the commander-in-chief. Indeed, the powers of the governor-general at last stood equal to his responsibilities.

This plan was admirably suited to the political position both in London and India, and lasted in essentials until 1858, by which time the Company had conquered India.

The first opportunity of wielding the new powers was given in 1786 to Cornwallis, an experienced soldier and administrator, a wise choice in the circumstances, for in the unstable position in India war was always likely to break out, and the Company was in no state to resist attack. On leaving England he was advised "to adopt a pacific and defensive system based on the universal principle . . . that we are completely satisfied with the possessions we already have." Indeed it was as clear in

London as in Bengal that the whole of its administration needed a thorough overhaul and, during the following ten years under Cornwallis and his successor, Shore, this was done and the foundations of a just, honest and efficient system laid. This, along with the accompanying settlement of the Government's chief source of income, the land revenue, formed not only the springboard from which the Company could leap at its enemies but also its justification for so doing; for they in comparison had nothing to offer India except the pursuit of personal power and endless war.

The most forceful of the Company's rivals, Tipu Sultan, who had succeeded his father, Haidar Ali, in Mysore, was for a time held at bay but by 1798, when Wellesley arrived as governor-general in India, the climax and clash of opposing forces was clearly at hand. Both Britain and India could hardly have been more fortunate in the personality of the governor-general at this juncture, for Wellesley, who was a friend and colleague of the British Prime Minister, William Pitt, took a far-sighted, world-wide view of events. For him the war against the French—which had started in 1793 and was to last until 1815, and which was to develop into the war against Napoleon's militarism—was the thing that mattered most, and seen in retrospect, his policy is justifiable in terms of both Europe and India. His vision was matched by his energy, ability and decisiveness in action, and he reached Calcutta with the words of Dundas, the British war minister, ringing in his ears, "If we choose we can be the arbiters of India."

By this time Napoleon's plans for the conquest of the Middle East were becoming known. He and his troops had already landed in Egypt and, to prepare for his advance eastwards, French agents had been despatched to the Sherif of Mecca and the Imam of Muscat, both Muslim rulers who could help to secure his possible line of communications; also to the French Governor of Mauritius warning him of Napoleon's approach, and to Tipu Sultan of Mysore as the ally of the French in India.

Tipu himself had recently solicited an alliance with France and had actually secured the despatch of a small French force from Mauritius. Even so, had Tipu's power formed the only base of a possible French attack, Wellesley, who had recently been reinforced by ships and men from home, could have contained or destroyed the threat without great difficulty, but in fact French officers were established also at Hyderabad, where they were training an army of sepoys, and among the Marathas, where two of them, de Boigne and Perron, successively commanded the armies of Sindhia, the leading Maratha chief.

The danger facing Wellesley was that the French might achieve a coalition, and he therefore sought to forestall Napoleon by isolating and, if necessary, destroying his possible allies one by one.

The Nizam of Hyderabad was the weakest and easiest to approach, and, by a mixed policy of promises and threats, Wellesley soon induced him to dismiss his French officers and accept English forces in their place. The way was thus opened for a trial of strength with Tipu. Dundas in London was urging, "If Tipu has made preparations of a hostile nature, or if the proclamation of Tipu inviting the French was his own, do not wait for actual hostilities on his part . . . attack him!", and Wellesley promptly called on him to abandon the French alliance.

Tipu's ambitions, however, ran counter to the existence of the British power in India, and he therefore accepted the challenge. In the campaign that followed his territories were overrun, his fortress of Seringapatam stormed and he himself slain, and in the treaty of settlement a reduced state of Mysore was handed over to the former ruling Hindu dynasty, which was friendly to and under the control of the British. An accompanying change of ruler and policy in the Carnatic, and a similar treaty with the ruler of Tanjore in the same region, left the Company by 1800 in virtual control of the entire peninsula south of the Marathas. Thus further French threats in India could take effect only through the Marathas and in the north.

Meanwhile, Nelson's naval victory at the Battle of the Nile off the coast of Egypt followed by the British defence of Acre pinned down the French in the Near East and forced Napoleon to abandon his eastern projects and return to France. Had

D

he persisted he would in all probability have met with disaster, for a British naval squadron from Bombay had been sent to patrol the narrow exit from the Red Sea and, as a gesture of confidence, Wellesley actually despatched a small British-Indian land force to assist in expelling the French from Egypt, whilst, at the courts of Persia and Muscat, British agents countered French diplomacy. French designs of controlling the land route to India therefore appeared to have been completely defeated, but Wellesley saw no reason why he should abandon his plans for destroying the hostile Maratha power.

Already he had revised the Company's relations with its weak and maladministered buffer state of Oudh, much reducing it in size and pushing the Company's territory farther up the Ganges valley until it made contact with the north-eastern frontiers of the Maratha lands. Just as he had first isolated before destroying Tipu, so Wellesley also began to drive wedges between the Maratha chiefs. Unfortunately for themselves, quite blind to the need and advantage of standing together, they played completely into his hands. Their titular head, the Peshwa, even sought British protection against his rivals, and Wellesley's armies, brilliantly led by Lord Lake and by his own brother, later the Duke of Wellington, found little difficulty in dealing with them as they came forward one by one.

Thus far Wellesley had received strong backing from home. Thanks to Britain's command of European and Eastern waters, a steady flow of reinforcements and large supplies, especially of bullion, had reached him. But as his demands rose and his future plans, for example, for a vast increase in the Company's armies, became more and more ambitious, the home authorities became anxious. Castlereagh, at this time in charge of Indian affairs in London, gave vent to his uneasiness—"I have very considerable doubts of your policy . . . extension of territory is too visible . . . it bears the feature of a systematic purpose of extending our territories in defiance of the recorded sense of Parliament." Already a large proportion of the profits of the Company's trade with China had been diverted to support the costs of territorial administration in India and, when it became apparent that Wellesley was also using for his war machine money originally supplied from England specifically to develop their Indian trade, the Company's directors lost all patience and recalled him. He came home to join his friends in cursing the directors—"those worthy cheesemongers," "those paltry shabroons," "those mean-spirited men," whose policy, so he maintained, was always governed "by the narrow view of commercial habits," —and although the directors rightly retorted that "there never was a more stale and unjust imputation," a fashion of prejudiced criticism against them was started which unhappily has persisted down to the present day.

Unfortunately, although Wellesley had broken the power of the Marathas, a peace was hastily patched up after his departure which left them crippled indeed but still a menace to the life of Central India. Wellesley had himself to blame: his successes had gone to his head and he had clearly exceeded his instructions, and overstrained the Company's resources. But his general achievement was magnificent. He was an avowed imperialist, seeing clearly that for Indians the political alternative was not British dominion or Indian independence, but rather the choice of French or British suzerainty over India; and, although Napoleon continued to devise vague plans and coalitions for attacking India and from time to time sent out agents, Wellesley in effect had settled this issue.

When final victory over Napoleon came in 1815 Britain retained possession of the Cape, Ceylon, Mauritius and the Seychelles Islands, and soon afterwards acquired Aden and, through the genius of Sir Stamford Raffles followed by negotiation with the Dutch, Singapore also. Thus the strategic design of controlling all the entrances into the Indian Ocean, as sound to-day as when it was first propounded by the Portuguese in the sixteenth century, was completely achieved by Britain, and so long as this position was maintained, that is until the fall of Singapore in 1942, British naval power safeguarded India from attack by sea. The struggle between the English and French in India, first begun in 1744, was therefore quite decided by 1815.

4. THE BRITISH ADVANCE TO THE NORTH-WEST AND "THE RUSSIAN MENACE"

The impossibility of standing indefinitely on the frontiers established by Wellesley soon became clear, and the task of clearing the flanks of the Company's northern territories devolved on Lord Hastings, governor-general between 1813 and 1823. At the beginning of his rule he reported home, "Within British territories all is quiet and well. On their borders the spirit is not so placid. Breaches, not formidable but likely to be very troublesome, have been postponed by management till the palliatives will serve no longer." Both to north and south of the Company's most populous and fertile territory in the Ganges valley the frontiers were constantly crossed by raiding forces.

In the north a brief war followed by a generous peace settled relations with the sturdy hill people of Nepal, but in the south the danger was much more serious. There enormous hordes of freebooters called Pindaris, by-products of the prolonged state of war and disorder in Maratha lands, had banded themselves into powerful irregular armies and, under the not unfriendly eyes of the Maratha chiefs, ransacked far and wide. Their continued existence was intolerable, but they could not be annihilated without also finally subjecting the Maratha states. This Hastings did between 1817-18, the Maratha chiefs to the end preferring through suspicion of one another to perish singly rather than combine.

Large territorial rearrangements followed, creating the modern Presidency of Bombay; and the peace signed with the Marathas brought the last of the important Indian rulers into treaty relations with the British. Indeed the Company had always been willing to recognize Indian princes who showed willingness to work and fight with them, with the consequence that they had entered from time to time, as circumstances dictated, into treaties bewildering in their variety, some, for example, authorizing the Company's interference in every sphere of internal and external policy, others merely enjoining mutual friendliness. However, taken together they established the Company's predominance and marked the first stage in the political re-integration of India.

The existence of the treaties did not as a matter of course

guarantee the inviolability of the Indian States. There was always a tendency, natural enough in the circumstances, to read the treaties together and interpret them into one clear-cut policy. Moreover, for a state in the Company's position, always subject to the influence of ideas current in Britain, not least those of the Evangelicals, the problem of outright annexation of territory arose every time there occurred in India a direct clash of eastern and western standards in government. Two considerable states were thus annexed during the governor-generalship of Dalhousie (1848–56), the one, Nagpur, when its ruler died without a son; the other, Oudh, which had long been shockingly misgoverned.

Meanwhile the more thoughtful and far-sighted of the Company's rulers had become increasingly concerned with the indefensibility of the Company's north-west and north-east frontiers. In Assam on the north-east an irresponsible Burmese government maintained a cruel tyranny, which was ignored by the Company until, in 1823, the Burmese king with characteristic but ignorant foolishness despatched a force into Bengal with orders to take Calcutta. In the war that followed the Burmese forces were easily overcome, and Assam and some parts of Burma were ceded to the Company, so that the frontier was pushed to mountainous, difficult but defensible country.

In the north-west the Company's frontier lay along the River Sutlej, well over a thousand miles from its main base at Calcutta. Here the problem was much more difficult. The Company, like all other strong, orderly powers in the midst of smaller, irregularly governed states, constantly felt the inclination to expand, but to drive farther to the north-west was to complicate an already slow communication system in which the bullock cart with its "cruising speed" of three miles an hour still played an essential part. However, experience from time immemorial had shown that a conquest of India which did not include occupation or control of the north-western passes into India was short-lived. Equally true was it that successful invasions of India were always possible to a power which could establish itself in the region we now call Afghanistan. And from about 1830 onwards it seemed clear to British statesmen, who still remembered Napoleon's plans for attacking India by land, that the Russian Government aimed at occupying this vital area.

In Europe, Russia and Britain did not see eye to eye, and, as the years passed, it became clear that in striving to put direct pressure on Britain, which was extremely difficult in Europe itself, the impulse of Russian policy against Britain tended to flow backwards and forwards between Europe and Central Asia. In 1828 Russian troops moving down the east coast of the Caspian Sea inflicted a heavy defeat on the Persians, and, after a short pause, they joined forces to threaten Afghanistan.

A glance at a large-scale map of Central Asia, revealing the enormous distances and difficult country to be covered, quickly dispels the notion that at this time Russia sought to launch a direct military attack on India, but she evidently intended, by a skilful variation of her pressure on Afghanistan and threat to India, to influence British policy in Europe itself. In this she succeeded, for British statesmen, both in London and Calcutta, apparently not given to the study of large-scale maps, proved unduly sensitive to "the Russian menace," as they termed it. As early as 1828 Lord Ellenborough, a member of the Cabinet and responsible for Indian affairs, opined that the British would have to fight the Russians on the Indus. Certainly in this, as in many other instances, vague national fears constituted the most powerful promoter of aggressive war.

It was true, as Ellenborough pointed out, that the British on their Sutlej frontier were badly placed for countering Russian agents in Afghanistan. Separating the two powers and controlling the routes to Kandahar and Kabul, lay a group of independent Indian states: in Sind in the lower Indus valley a family of chieftains, collectively known as the Amirs, looked to the north-west rather than into India for political support, and farther north in the Punjab a formidable warrior chief, Ranjit Singh, had coerced the Sikh clans into a united fighting force. Although he respected and lived at peace with the Company it was obvious that on his death instability would follow, for only a man of his outstanding gifts could maintain intact both his own position and the Sikh state: and in his family there was only one Ranjit Singh.

In these circumstances anxiety in London drove the Company into taking a series of false steps. Had Lord Auckland, the unfortunate governor-general of the day, been a stronger personality disaster might have been avoided, but, as it was, after trying in vain in 1837 to bring the ruler of Afghanistan under his diplomatic control, he allowed himself to be pushed into an attempt forcibly to establish the Company's nominee on the throne of Kabul. Lacking full control of the Indus Valley, through which his essential line of communications ran, Auckland's attempt was doomed to failure and in fact in the First Afghan War (1838–43) his forces were annihilated. The Company's prestige for the first time since Plassey suffered a severe blow and the Amirs of Sind felt emboldened openly to resent the free use of their territory. To crown all, in 1839, Ranjit Singh died.

With little justification, except that of military necessity, Lord Ellenborough, who had succeeded Auckland, annexed Sind, thus placing the British within direct reach of Afghanistan and strategically outflanking the Sikhs. With both parties afraid of each other, war inevitably followed and, in a series of bloody battles between 1845 and 1849, was fought out in the Company's favour. The Punjab was then annexed, and the last of the land frontiers of British India pushed from the plains into the defensible mountains.

. . . . .

Thus in just over a century the East India Company had conquered India and made its peoples safe against external attack. Indeed, with India in political and military dissolution and European traders settled on her coasts, the world-wide rivalry of European powers had made some attempt at conquest inevitable. It happened to be a British conquest because they alone both understood and applied the Portuguese strategy in dominating the Indian seas and the French technique in subjecting the mainland. Although it formed a magnificent achievement, it had not been deliberately planned and pursued: no Briton was as wise and far-seeing as that! Once on the move it was difficult for the Company to find a secure frontier: the home authorities, even Parliament, hoping to force a halt, frequently forbade further conquest, but fear, that powerful stimulus of aggressive war, proved far stronger; fear of the French, of Mysore, of the Marathas; fear of the Sikhs, fear of Russia drew the Company's armies across India to the Himalayas. A critic of the Company's directors, with some appearance of truth, could and did say, "The regular system for the last thirty or forty years has been to lament over the act of expansion and to pocket the income. You have doubled your territories while you have been delivering your morals," but, in fact, the directors were sincerely, if mistakenly, persuaded that—in their own words —"our dominion is not so well served by vast extent and by bridling all the courts of Hindustan, as it would have been by a more moderate and compact territory and leaving the other states to themselves." But in India of the eighteenth and nineteenth centuries, as in the world to-day, they found that peace was indivisible.

The Company always recognized that its continued existence in India depended on its armies, and it was the more extraordinary, therefore, that in its forces only a small percentage of British troops was employed, the bulk being made up of sepoys usually in the proportion of five or six to one European. Success in this policy was made possible only by an adequate and certain payment of these troops—a condition incidentally almost unknown among the Company's rivals—which again depended on the development and maintenance of a regular and expanding financial and administrative system.

Even then it was found that the costs of governing its Indian territories exceeded the income from them so that further progress was often achieved only by drawing on the profits of the Company's China trade. Certainly in paying its way from 1784 onwards no large scale exploitation of India *by the Company* took place for in that year its profits, in point of fact usually made on the China trade, were limited to eight per cent by law, and in 1813 Parliament forced the Company to give up its India trade altogether.

The military conquest and administrative unification of India by the East India Company represents one of mankind's great achievements: without it, the British political reintegration of India would not have been possible.

CHAPTER III

THE MEANING OF THE
EAST INDIA COMPANY'S RULE

I. POLITICAL AND ECONOMIC UNIFICATION

IN assessing the value of the Company's rule in India we must never forget that it succeeded to an empire that had rotted away through half a century of growing turbulence. Every man who could gather an army was busy carving out a state for himself, and bent on destroying his nearest rivals and, amidst the marching and counter-marching of armies, the life of the villager and townsman alike had become more miserably insecure than for two centuries past. Sustained economic and cultural development had ceased and political morality degenerated with the times. In the words of an Indian historian, "Mean intrigue and treacherous conspiracy were the very breath of the life of the nobles and officers, and violation of plighted word, perfidy and assassination were common occurrences with our rulers of the first half of the eighteenth century."

On this chaotic scene the Company gradually imposed order and political unity and established standards both in law and conduct, which, although not always of the highest, were yet immeasurably higher than those they replaced. And through the Company's experiments in government there evolved and was first applied the principle that trusteeship —which might lead to partnership—formed the proper relationship between stronger and weaker peoples.

With the spread of order was reborn a sense of security and the possibility of a continued recovery in agriculture, which, to a country of peasants like India, at first constituted the greatest single boon that could be offered. These achievements were deliberately worked for by the Company's leaders, but the most penetrating and widespread changes, those in the total economic life of India, were not consciously sought by the Company's government but rather brought about by the interaction of overwhelming world-wide forces which the British conquest let loose in India.

For over thirty centuries the economic life of India had hardly changed. The village society was absorbed in agriculture and, sometimes with sometimes without the co-operation of the central authority of the day, strove to make life easier by supplementing the essential but uncertain rains with irrigation works: its main concern therefore was with land rather than trade, and the village organization, with purely local markets and restricted purchasing power, unchangingly remained the norm.

On the triumph of the Company a ruling power with a vested interest in developing trade for the first time took charge of India, and the new industrial towns of Britain, with all the power of the technological revolution behind them, became supreme alike over the English and Indian countryside. Indian merchants, comparable in resources and ability with those of London and Amsterdam, had long thrived in Indian ports—one of them, for example, Virji Vora of Surat being renowned as the richest in the world—but they had touched only the fringe of Indian life, whereas British traders carrying a superabundance of manufactures, especially of cotton goods, penetrated along the main arteries of communication and, with the Company's government sweeping away all trade barriers in British territory, seeped through the villages into the heart of Indian life. The Indian weaving industry, long the nucleus of India's export trade, was steadily overwhelmed, as indeed were many of her other old trades and crafts such as metalworking and glass-making, and considerable numbers of craftsmen were thrown out of work.

Down to 1813 the Company retained its original grant of the monopoly of British trade with India but, by that year, the new and clamorous private trading interests, which had been gathering strength in the House of Commons, could no longer be denied and India was opened to them all: in 1833 the profitable China trade monopoly was also yielded in the face of similar pressure, the Company thus ceasing altogether to be a trading concern. Not so much, therefore, through a deliberate policy of exploitation directed by the Government in London as through the combination in India of immense British political and economic power, India became a vast, dependent market for Britain: inevitably she suffered, but in the process was slowly revitalized and changed from a static into a dynamic civilization.

Just as in trade the Company was forced to give way to a greater economic force than itself, so also in government it had to accept the supervision of the British Parliament. Throughout its history the Company had been attacked in the House of Commons by rival and jealous London trading groups and when, in Clive's time, it became territorially powerful in Madras and Bengal, the clamour grew and much of the criticism could no longer be gainsaid. The Company, indeed, in that first slice into India, quick as a knife through cheese, did not foresee—indeed hardly had the time to foresee—the consequences of wielding military power without accepting political responsibility. Her servants had gone to India, not for their health, but to make fortunes and most of them naturally enough were more interested in their own private trade than in the Company's good name, and they seized their financial opportunities. In Bengal, for instance, Clive and his officers fell in with the Indian custom of accepting enormous gifts; in Madras, through a cunning initial loan of money at high interest to the Nawab of Arcot, a group of swindlers, of whom Paul Benfield was the most notorious, finally held a whole province to ransom. The Company could hardly have made a worse beginning.

The news of these events, the hectic fluctuation in India stock, and the appearance in Bath and London of these *nouveaux riches* from India, the "Nabobs" as they were called, in particular their tendency to buy their way and that of their friends into Parliament, aroused in the English ruling classes that most potent mixture of feelings, envy and alarm. Soon after his return to London, Clive was called to account before the Commons for his actions in Bengal, and, although acquitted, it became clear that many members of the House felt that, through the East India Company, Britain had in fact assumed without as yet exercising a responsibility in India. This view was implied in the passing of an Act in 1773 to regulate the Company's affairs, but this unfortunately left the responsibility within the Company so divided and vaguely defined that Warren Hastings, appointed by the Act as the first governor-general of the Company's scattered Indian territories, was driven to the most doubtful expedients both in raising money and in maintaining his authority. In consequence the whole position had to be clarified in Pitt's India Acts of 1784 and 1786, and in them Britain plainly avowed a moral responsibility for the Company's rule in India. Henceforth the Company's governments in London and India were supervised by a minister of the Crown—the President of the Board of Control as he was named—who was responsible to the Cabinet and Parliament; and this system lasted down to 1858. Unfortunately the decision was taken at the same time to impeach Hastings but, although he was finally acquitted, it would have been juster if the framers of the vague, contradictory Act of 1773 and not Hastings had been put in the dock.

2. ADMINISTRATIVE UNIFICATION

Warren Hastings was the first Englishman seriously to weigh in the balance the relative merits of different systems of administering the Company's new conquests.

The whole province of Bengal lay under the military control of the Company, but a few hundreds of British traders and soldiers could hardly be expected promptly to assume the administration of a population numbering millions, whose language even they hardly understood; and their only alternative at first was to accept a hand-to-mouth policy and allow the Indian ruler, the Nawab, and his ministers, to carry on. This system of indirect control led to such confusion and delay and offered such opportunities for double-dealing that the Company's directors in London, on appointing Warren Hastings as Governor of Bengal in 1772, instructed him at once to put an end to the policy of dual control and to assume full responsibility for every branch of the administration.

Hastings took over at the worst possible time. Not only was the Company threatened by the French and rival Indian states, but Bengal itself in 1770 had been devastated by famine under the strain of which all government had broken down. Moreover, all systems depend for their success on the persons who work them and the quality of his civil assistants was not high: nominated in their teens by one or other of the twenty-four Company directors in London, and according to rank bearing the title of writer, factor, junior or senior merchant, they had come to India avowedly to profit through trade. Hastings' task and achievement essentially consisted in maintaining the Company's territories against attack and at the same time turning a commercial organization into the government of a province. Only a man of genius could have done it, and although necessarily rough-hewn his work was guided by remarkable knowledge and insight.

The Company's position rested on the army, whose efficiency, like that of most armies, largely depended in turn on the receipt of regular pay. Under the Nawab, however, payments had been anything but regular, and Hastings therefore rightly chose to deal with the financial problem first.

Indian governments traditionally drew their income from the land, largely in the form of land revenue taken yearly as that share of the peasant's produce which was held to be due to the state; and this might amount to one-third or even one-half of the total produce. The Company in 1772 under its new policy of assuming the government of Bengal was therefore obliged for the first time both to assess and collect this revenue; but standing between them and the peasants was a large group of landholders, or zamindars as they were called, who by custom undertook these tasks for the state in return for a share of the amount collected. The zamindars, however, had already roused suspicions that they were using their intermediary position to oppress the peasants and defraud the Company, and Hastings, taking advantage of the state's traditional right to change the whole system, decided on the bold experiment of dismissing the existing zamindars and auctioning their posts. Such a plan might have succeeded in more settled times, but the grave dislocation of agriculture caused by the recent famine would have made nonsense of any land reform, and in effect all that Hastings succeeded in doing was to set the Company the impossible task of gathering the revenue from the speculators who had rushed to buy the zamindars' posts in the hope of extorting what they could from the peasantry. Hastings therefore failed in his main aim of discovering the worth of the zamindars' services, and after persisting for five years, he gave up the plan. Henceforth, prudently refusing to commit himself to any one system, he tried various experiments in order to collect much needed information about the land revenue system as a whole. Undoubtedly right in beginning with financial reform, Hastings seems to have been over-anxious to achieve a settled system: but from his failures and experiments his successors were to benefit.

In revising the system of law courts, thus bringing a rough justice within reach of the people of the province for the first time in two generations, Hastings was much more successful. Basing all he did on current Indian practice in Bengal he defined precisely two sets of local courts, each with a considerable degree of executive power, one to deal with matters affecting the public peace, the other with revenue cases and all civil disputes. In criminal matters appeal was allowed to the titular Nawab, in civil matters to the Governor-General in Council, and despite some difficulties arising from a clash of jurisdiction with the Supreme Court established by the Regulating Act of 1773, the system worked splendidly and became popular with the people. Not that it was perfect in itself, but it represented another step forward on the road from anarchy to law and order.

From all that Hastings did it is evident that he desired above all to fuse the Indian and the Company's forms of government into a system suited to the circumstances. It did not occur to him to attempt to import a completely English system of administration: indeed, he would have dismissed as nonsensical such a project in a country so dissimilar from England. To him, with his wide knowledge of India and deep insight into the problems of governing a foreign people, it seemed possible to revise Indian personal methods of rule in such a way that a joint staff of Indians and English could manage the new administrative machine. His plan could hardly have established itself because a succession of men with Hastings' own qualities and attitude of mind would have been needed to supervise it; but in any event viewed from London it appeared merely to be a clever design on Hastings' part to establish himself as an oriental potentate with despotic authority.

The India Act of 1784, followed by the impeachment of Hastings, showed that the British Parliament had rejected his ideas of government: henceforth, the governors-general were almost always chosen from English political life, and the first of them, Cornwallis, a tried and trusted servant of the Crown, was sent to India in 1786 to reorganize the Company's system in conformity with the ideas expressed in London.

A more fitting choice for this purpose than Cornwallis could hardly have been made. A landed gentleman, English to the backbone and proud of his heritage, he was convinced that English ways were right and best. Personally honest and just, and firm in self-discipline no matter in what country or situation he found himself, he was accustomed to demand the same standards of others. He sailed from an England in which the teachings of Adam Smith, the great economist, were becoming increasingly accepted, particularly the view, most attractive to a soldier's mind, that in government simplicity and certainty were above all desirable.

He disliked on sight what he found of Hastings' administration, especially the heritage of Indian forms of government and the large degree of executive power vested in the Company's revenue collectors as compared with the limited jurisdiction of the judges, and he systematically set to work to devise a more straightforward, uniform and English system of administration, finally summing up all he had done by 1793 in a code of Regulations which put a stamp on Indian government that can be clearly seen to-day.

It seemed to Cornwallis that so long as a fresh assessment and collection of the land revenue had to be made each year most of the Company's officials would continue to be absorbed in this work, for which they would also need wide discretionary powers; but that if a permanent settlement of the land revenue were announced, the system at one stroke would become clear and simple, and the Company's senior servants be freed for the vastly more important task in his eyes of administering justice.

After long deliberation he took this decision—which has been adhered to ever since—and at the same time made it clear that he was disposed to regard the intermediary class of zamindars as landlords in the English sense, thus in effect transforming their right to a share in the produce of the land into a claim to the land itself. The consequences did not at once become obvious, but it is now clear that a grave injustice was done to the peasants: moreover the state had alienated in advance the main source from which an increase in the state income could in future be expected, and in fact through the nineteenth century the land of Bengal steadily rose in value. Lastly, once the Permanent Settlement was made, punctual payment was demanded from the zamindars, failing which their rights were auctioned. In this way many long-established landholders were displaced by mere speculators, at once a burden on the peasants and a menace to the state.

But there was no denying the simplicity and certainty of the plan and its conformity with English ideas, and with equal determination Cornwallis introduced these characteristics into the whole administration. It was his conviction—to which force was given by the appallingly low standard of Indian public life—that an English system could be effectively conducted only by Englishmen, and to the Company's servants therefore were reserved all the higher civil posts, excepting the governorships which were usually filled from England, and an accompanying act of Parliament defined these higher posts as carrying a yearly salary of £800 and more. A decade later the imperialist, Wellesley, with his usual foresight and vigour, and perhaps developing an earlier proposal of Warren Hastings, decided that his civil servants ought to be trained for their jobs, and finally Haileybury College in England was established for the purpose. Honesty and efficiency were thus to form the twin pillars of the administration.

Although the more enlightened of the Company's servants, such as Thomas Munro and John Malcolm, later denounced the policy of excluding Indians from the higher posts the ideas elaborated by Cornwallis, and firmly supported by the London authorities, became too deeply embedded in the system to be easily removed: the British Parliament might declare in 1833, and the Crown repeat in 1858, that all races and creeds should be freely admitted "to Our service," but the system easily prevailed against mere words. Munro and Malcolm, indeed, had wished to give Indians "a higher opinion of themselves by employing them in important situations," but the Indians they had in mind were clearly those whom they would have termed "the natural leaders," the princes and chiefs and landed aristocracy: they certainly did not foresee, any more than the Government, the growth of a quite different Indian class, the urban middle-class intelligentsia, which ultimately made nonsense of the unduly prolonged application of Cornwallis's policy.

To protect his officials against the possibility of corruption Cornwallis increased their salaries, and firmly separated the Company's commercial and territorial branches, the first under the control of a Board of Trade, the second under the more important Board of Revenue. The latter's task was to supervise the work of the officers in the local districts, the administrative units into which all Bengal was divided; and on the relative importance of their work Cornwallis differed from Hastings.

Within each district the Company undertook three essential functions, to keep the peace, to collect the revenues, to administer justice. To Warren Hastings the collectors, whose duties kept them in close touch with the people, had been the key figures, but to Cornwallis the judges, behind whom stood the Law, ranked pre-eminent; and although for a time all three main functions were combined in one official, Cornwallis finally made the judge a separate and superior figure, and gave him control of the police. The law administered in the local courts continued, as under Hastings, to be the existing law, whether Hindu or Muslim, requiring as time went on clarification and codification, but the spirit animating it was English and, therefore, in this context, revolutionary, substituting for the arbitrary interpretations and orders of an individual the settled principles of a system universally applied.

It was hardly to be expected that the people would understand the significance of these changes—much of the new system, indeed, must have seemed to them mere mumbo-

E

jumbo—and around the courts a large class of professional lawyers and, what was much worse, of professional witnesses, sprang up, between them confusing and making expensive the processes of justice. Most serious of all, the deliberate procedures adopted and the large number of cases arising through the land revenue changes, made the system slow, sometimes impossibly so, and by 1812, for example, the arrears of cases in the courts of Bengal numbered over 163,000, which in effect amounted to a denial of justice.

Fortunately in the Presidencies of Madras and Bombay, even though Wellesley made an attempt to apply the Cornwallis system, it was possible to avoid the worst of the errors committed in Bengal. On the one hand the home authorities soon drew the right conclusions from the Company's administrative experience in Bengal, and on the other local conditions in Madras and Bombay were quite different and thus demanded different treatment. Most important of all, no class of land-holders similar to the zamindars of Bengal intervened between the Government and the ryots, or peasants. The former, therefore, through its collectors was driven to making a direct assessment and collection of the cultivators' land revenue.

This ryotwari system, as it was called, imposed a great deal of work on the Company's local officers, but unlike the zamindari system in Bengal in which the judge was just as tied to his court as the collector to his office, it kept the collector, and indirectly the Government, in close touch with the people. Because he knew best what was going on in the countryside, the collector also retained control of the police, a method of maintaining order so much more effective than the Bengal plan of giving the judges this responsibility that it later came to be typical of British India as a whole, ultimately being adopted in Bengal itself.

In the areas in the Upper Ganges and Indus valleys which fell under British control in the second quarter of the nineteenth century, thanks largely to the wisdom of the London directors, who saw that the Bengal system was likely to make the Government almost inaccessible to Indian opinion, no serious attempt was made either to extend the Bengal regulations and system of law courts or to distinguish sharply between the judges and the executive officials. Instead a more personal mode of rule, termed the Non-Regulation System, was adopted. This, similar to former Indian practice, united the more important functions of government in each district in one person, a deputy commissioner, whilst still insisting on the observance of a rule of law by officials and people alike, and it proved highly successful from the points of view of both governors and governed. In the 1830's the Company's administrative system throughout northern India was severely tested by the decision to identify, track down and exterminate the large gangs of professional assassins, called Thugs, who under a Hindu religious sanction had long existed and defied earlier governments. It came triumphantly through the ordeal.

Despite all the defects of the Cornwallis system—and most of them arose from his haste in applying so alien a method of administration to a people of whom the British knew so little— the salient ideas of introducing a Rule of Law and insisting on a respect for law were obviously good. They contained within them the germ of the principle of trusteeship and, to a country like India, split into so many heterogeneous communities, certainly constitute one of the Company's greatest gifts.

3. EUROPEAN INFLUENCES

It was inevitable that, through an English system of administration, English ideas would exert a determining influence on the course of Indian policy. The Company might struggle, for example, to preserve its monopoly of Indian trade and protect the Indian merchant and craftsman, but it failed completely to prevent the absorption of its territories into the British free trade area. The Company might also begin by declaring that the Indians would tolerate its rule only if their religions and customs were left untouched, and that Christian missionaries must therefore be excluded from India, but it had yet to face the fact that one of the strongest influences running through the British Parliament of the first half of the nineteenth century was reformist and that in the vanguard of the reformers stood the Evangelicals under William Wilberforce. Several of his group, the "Saints" as they were called, also had seats in the Company's Court of Directors. Charles Grant and Edward Parry, to mention two, were active, able men, well described by one critic as having "infinite kindness in their characters and mad only upon one subject—religion"; and certainly they were the more influential, and perhaps dangerous, because they were so sincerely convinced that they were the chosen instruments of Almighty God.

In the 1780's Warren Hastings had been able to accept Indians as they were, without a positive desire or plan to change them, but thirty years later, largely through the efforts of the "Saints," this attitude of mind was no longer permitted to a governor-general. In 1813, Wilberforce and his friends persuaded Parliament to allow missionaries to go to India and thenceforth the criticism both in India and England of all those aspects of Indian life which were shocking to English minds—and they were many—increased in volume and ferocity. Some of the immediate results were wholly beneficial; the Hindu practice of suttee, that is the self-immolation of widows on their husbands' pyres, a survival from the primitive origins of Hinduism, was prohibited by Lord William Bentinck, the governor-general, in 1829, despite the appeals to the Privy Council in London of a large body of Brahmans. In the same category fell the Company's veto of female infanticide, long practised among the Rajputs, and the abolition of slavery in 1843. But these reforms in fact touched only the fringe of Indian life, and by deliberate Company policy the essential structure of Hinduism was left untouched.

The fact that Englishmen could be so shocked by things Indian revealed some lack of understanding, but unfortunately their attitude even tended to be contemptuous, and in this Wilberforce set the standard: "Our Christian religion," he told the members of Parliament, "is sublime, pure and beneficent. The Indian religious system is mean, licentious and cruel . . . It is one grand abomination!" To him Hinduism was meaningless and therefore execrable, and sweeping criticism from this point of view, although it induced the Company to oppose the more obviously irrational and inhuman Indian customs, yet served fundamentally to antagonize the Indian world.

In religious policy the Company itself felt obliged to act with the greatest caution, but in educational matters, because the consequences were more difficult to foresee and the subject seemed to Englishmen of that day less dangerous and important and not the concern of the State, a much bolder line was in fact taken.

To some of the Company's servants of Warren Hastings' generation the revival of education in India had seemed desirable and—as one would expect from the zest with which they adopted Indian ways of living and learned their languages—they favoured not so much the introduction of English ideas but rather the revival of Hindu and Muslim learning through the classical Indian languages, Sanskrit and Persian. Failing any other positive point of view, this vague inclination in policy lingered on so that when in 1813, as an outcome of Wilberforce's work, the East India Company was authorized to spend some £10,000 yearly in spreading *useful learning* in India, the money at first went to maintain Sanskrit and Persian scholars and to translate useful text-books into those languages. Meanwhile a conflicting school of thought had arisen.

The application of Cornwallis's system of administration inevitably introduced English ideas and standards not only in political but also in religious and social matters. The Company's Indian governments soon found, for example, that they needed large numbers of subordinate clerks able to read and write English, and from 1826 onwards actually gave preference to junior appointments in the law courts to Indians possessing suitable English certificates. In the following year the directors told the governor-general that "the first object of improved education should be to prepare a body of individuals for discharging public duties," and simultaneously it appeared that numbers of Indians, in Calcutta especially but also in Bombay and Madras, were asking for nothing better than to be so trained. Among Hindus and Muslims generally literacy was not regarded as a necessary training for life but rather as a means to certain vocations such as the priesthood and government office. Earlier to make sure of state employment many Hindus among the Brahman and writer castes, who had a literate tradition, had not hesitated to learn Persian when the

Muslims conquered and began to administer India, and their descendants, whose regular livelihood was drawn from the public service, were equally eager to learn English. The Muslims, on the other hand, resentful of their recent displacement from power, hung back with the disastrous consequence that they lost so much educational ground that even to-day they have not fully been able to make up.

The Christian missionaries—whose general viewpoint at this time may perhaps best be summarized in Charles Grant's words, "The cure of darkness is light!"—at once saw their opportunity and, confident that the introduction of Indians to the study of English would achieve their twofold purpose of undermining Hinduism and extending Christianity, began to open schools giving not merely a vocational training but a general education on English lines. In Bombay the Parsi community, which dominated the economic life of the city, welcomed this development: in Madras, English was rapidly adopted as a *lingua franca*; but it was in Calcutta, where two colleges were established before 1820, that the greatest advance was made.

This conjunction of public need and private impulse determined from the start the main lines of the Company's educational policy, but great stress is usually laid on the alleged decisive influence of Thomas Babington Macaulay's famous Minute on Education of February, 1835, which urged the extension among Indians of western knowledge exclusively through the English language. Characteristically he wrote this within a few weeks of his arriving at Calcutta to take his seat as legal adviser on the Governor-General's Council, and when his first-hand knowledge of India was still slight.

It is quite clear, however, that the circumstances were such that if Macaulay had never gone to India, if his Minute on Education had never been written, the same decision would in fact have been upheld by the Company. Macaulay's Minute is important rather because of the scornful attitude to Indian culture revealed in it. So cocksure was his argument that, after admitting "I have no knowledge of either Sanskrit or Arabic," he declared, "I have never found one among the Orientalists who could deny that a single shelf of a good European library was worth the whole native literature of India and Arabia. . . . It is, I believe, no exaggeration to say that all the historical information which has been collected from all the books written in the Sanskrit language is less valuable than what may be found in the most paltry abridgements used at preparatory schools in England." Throughout the argument sneer followed sneer: "Medical doctrines which would disgrace an English farrier, astronomy which would move laughter in girls at an English boarding school, history abounding with kings thirty feet high and reigns thirty thousand years long, and geography made up of seas of treacle and seas of butter." Thus with a succession of half-truths he dismissed Indian culture.

This contemptuous attitude of mind, first implied in Cornwallis's wholesale anglicization of the Company's administration, then supported by Wilberforce's reaction to Hinduism, and capped by Macaulay's complete condemnation of Indian cultures, was representative of an influential section of English opinion throughout the nineteenth and early twentieth centuries; and it largely accounts for the general English lack of interest in things Indian and, despite a close association of two hundred years, a comparative neglect in Britain of Indian studies. When, towards the close of the nineteenth century, Indians began to examine the implications of this attitude, particularly that of racial inferiority, many were irrevocably antagonized and moved to retaliate in ways which have radically affected Indo-British relations and the course of Indian politics.

4. INDIAN REACTIONS

The immediate effects of teaching English to those who hoped to enter the lower ranks of the Company's service were profound. It was true that little of what they learnt filtered from them through the watertight compartments of Indian society and that the absence of a plan for female education severely limited its influence in the home, but within these limits the Indian students of English entered a new life. Taught by the missionaries to question the validity of their own sacred books and creeds, they questioned also the teachings and stories of the Bible, so that although they tended to abandon their own superstitions they did not at once accept, as the missionaries had hoped, a new and Christian framework of life. One of the first reactions was that groups of Indians, especially in Calcutta, began to discuss the reform of Hinduism, the breakdown of caste, the prevention of child marriage, and, with these ideas in mind, Ram Mohun Roy, the ablest and most prominent Bengali of his generation, formed a society, the Brahmo Samaj, which still continues and which has fathered numerous other reforming societies, the underlying assumption of most being that Hinduism possesses an inherent capacity to develop and reform itself.

In short, European influences, which had already revolutionized the political and economic life of India, began also to change the very texture of Indian thought and belief.

With this intellectual and religious renascence, which is still in progress, came a renascence of literature. Earlier Sanskrit literary forms had been mainly poetic, but the missionaries needed prose forms in the vernacular languages, partly to teach with, partly to present the Bible intelligibly; thus the Serampore missionaries, for example, founded Bengali prose, which was soon developed by Indians into a magnificent vehicle for conveying not only religious, but also political, social and artistic ideas. It was but a short step to the establishment of a vernacular press, and the first regular newspaper in Bengali began to be published in 1818.

An English press had been in existence in all three Presidency towns for at least a quarter of a century, and the strict control exercised over it by the Government was automatically extended to the vernacular press. But in 1835, in accordance with English ideas and on the analogy that what was fitting for England was fitting also for India, the press as a whole was freed from censorship. With a free and responsible government the press forms at once a means of expressing and influencing public opinion but, in the India of that time, public opinion could hardly be said to exist. Logically and intelligently the freeing of the press in British India should have proceeded step by step with the approach to constitutional government. As it was, under the Company's despotic government the freed press soon became an irresponsible opponent, acting not so much, as is often maintained, as a steam safety valve, but rather as extra fuel tossed into the furnace under the boiler; and the explosion in India took place suddenly in 1857.

.   .   .   .   .

The impact of English military and economic strength in India had toppled down most of the superstructure of the Indian political world; and the Company's continued policy of annexation, which reached its climax under Governor-General Dalhousie, followed by the application of an English system of administration, threatened its complete annihilation. Furthermore, the new intellectual renascence through English education, through the newspapers and the active preaching of Christian missionaries, began to break up the foundations of that world.

The Indian masses were not roused to active opposition any more than they had been when the Muslims invaded India, but the Indians of rank and learning, first made uneasy by the completeness of the political and economic conquest, were filled with alarm at the influences which continued to undermine their religion, whether Hindu or Muslim, and which in fact constituted a persistent attack on their way of life. The typical aloofness of their English rulers, combined with the contemptuous attitude which appeared to underlie all English policies, increased the breach between them and made it more difficult for the Company's governments to realize clearly what was happening in the minds and hearts of Indians.

Signs and symptoms of general unrest had appeared much earlier, particularly in the mutiny in 1807 of the sepoys at Vellore in the Madras Presidency. There the desire of the British commander-in-chief to introduce uniformity of appearance among his Indian troops led to orders affecting their distinguishing caste marks, the hair on their faces, and their dress and turbans. These changes, set against a background of exceptional activity by Christian missionaries and rumours of forced conversions to Christianity in South India, were interpreted by the sepoys as an attack on their religion, and, taking advantage of slack discipline, they finally mutinied: but the proportion of European troops in the neighbourhood was sufficiently high to enable the rising to be promptly crushed. The significance of this event lay in the fact that unrest among the general population in Madras had found expression through the only *organized* body of Indians in the south—the sepoy army.

In the completely unsettled state of the Indian world persistent interference with Indian customs was equivalent to sitting on a barrel of gunpowder and playing with a lighted match, and by 1857 the people of the northern plains were agog with resentments similar to those of Vellore, though mixed in even more explosive proportions.

Normally English troops in India stood to sepoys in the ratio of 1 to 3 but, on the outbreak of the Crimean war in 1854, withdrawals reduced it to about 1 to 8, a lower ratio than ever before, and this, too, at a time when the Company's military reputation had been shaken by the wars in Afghanistan and the Punjab. To general unrest among the peoples of the Ganges valley, who had most directly felt the impact of the Company's religious, social and educational policy, was added particular anger among the Oudh land-holders at the recent British annexation of that province. These resentments were focused in the only organized body of Indians in the north, the predominantly high caste Bengal sepoys in the Company's army which drew most of its recruits from Oudh, and, as in 1807, a series of false rumours that the British intended to break down the caste system touched off a train of explosions, the last and biggest of which occurred in May 1857.

This outbreak was much more than a mutiny of sepoys and much less than a national rebellion. The other organized bodies of Indians, the Madras and the Bombay sepoy armies, were hardly affected, and the Indian princes lifted not a finger to support the rebels. The mass of the people, as usual, remained quiescent. Thus confined in area and lacking leadership and singlemindedness the mutiny was quelled within a year, but its consequences for India dominated the quarter-century that followed. On both sides the fighting had been pitiless, the atrocities many, the Indian and British press, as might have been expected, blinded with hate and hysterical for revenge. Not even the restrained good sense of Queen Victoria's proclamation promising "unconditional pardon, amnesty and oblivion of all offence" could prevent the English in India from declaring that the lesson they must learn from the Mutiny was "Never again"; and they became more aloof, more contemptuous, more irresistible than ever, quickly pushing their strategic railways and telegraph lines from Calcutta to the north-west, down to Bombay and across to Madras. Unmistakably western influence would continue to play on India with increasing force. For later Indian generations, on the other hand, the lesson accepted was not that the Mutiny formed the last revolt of ancient India against the modern world, but rather the first beginnings of the Indian war of independence.

.   .   .   .   .

In 1858, as a direct consequence of the Mutiny, the Crown took from the East India Company the formal and direct responsibility for the government of India. The tragedy of the Mutiny was the greater in that it has obscured both for the British and Indians much of the undoubted magnificence and inspiration of the Company's achievement.

The Company's was certainly the strongest government that had ever ruled India; equally, and this has not always been appreciated, it was the most enlightened. Considering that through the Company European influences touched the most sensitive parts of Indian life it was a miracle that the Mutiny had not taken place much earlier. Only the extraordinary consistency and wisdom of its policy prevented this, and the part played by the home government in London should not be forgotten. Statesmen of the first cabinet rank took their turn in London at managing Indian affairs—Canning and Castlereagh to mention the two most eminent—but their horizon was the western world, and, as they usually found, nothing is so little useful as reasoning by analogy from Europe to India. Rather it was the Company's directors, most of them with service in India and hard-working, sober business men, who knew what they were about, and they unfortunately formed the particular target of abuse for misguided politicians. In uniformly opposing the Company's expansion in India the directors certainly went astray largely because they were sincerely, if wrongly, convinced that the Company could live at peace with its Indian neighbours however much the latter might fight among themselves. On most other important aspects of policy, however, the directors' considered views stand investigation and the test of time. The style preferred in their despatches may have been, as they said, "the humdrum" but the substance constitutes a magnificently wise code of the ethics of government.

The Company's rule may have rested continually upon the force of arms but through it, political and economic unity, a regular and honest administration, impartial justice, the extension of knowledge and the suppression of barbarous customs were imposed as part of the functions of the state, thus making possible later experiments in Indian representative government. This marked a great advance on the political ideas of previous Indian rulers who had mainly concerned themselves with large revenues, ever greater armies, and vaster states.

But the most fundamental change of all under the Company came about through the exposure of India's peoples to the full force of British industrial and commercial strength and of the religious, social and educational ideas of the West— forces strong beyond the Company's power to control—which turned a static into a dynamic civilization. A system of government is usually as good as the men who work it and, amidst the play of these mighty influences, the Company's system brought to the front a glorious series of able rulers: Warren Hastings, Wellesley, Elphinstone, Munro and Metcalfe, the Lawrences, and one could list a score such names. In them we see a succession of noble characters; of men who valued and knew how to achieve law and order and who worked for the political and spiritual reintegration of a united India; in them we see a true vision of greatness.

CHAPTER IV

THE GROWTH OF INDIAN NATIONALISM, 1858-1909

I. CONTINUITY IN BRITISH POLICY

THE disappearance of the East India Company in 1858 marked a change in the form of the government of India but not in the substance of policy. Queen Victoria's proclamation to the "Princes, Chiefs and Peoples of India," announcing the transfer of power to the Crown, expressly took up the threads of the Company's consistent policy, promising complete religious toleration and the maintenance of the "ancient rights, usages and customs of India"; and in the Act that followed it was laid down that "all acts and provisions now in force under charter or otherwise in India shall continue in force." Virtually the only change was the substitution at home of a Secretary of State with an India Council of fifteen members in place of the President of the Board of Control and the Court of Directors.

Plans under preparation and discussion before and during the Mutiny were quickly carried into effect. The Company's covenanted civil service became the Indian Civil Service, recruited on the method of open competitive examination in London—first introduced in 1853 to replace the system of nomination. The Company's three armies were treated as one, for which henceforth British troops were not to be recruited. Instead, "The army in India" was to be made up of Indian troops commanded by British officers serving permanently, and of units from the British army on a temporary tour of duty.

Extensive law reforms, announcing the end of the Company's dual system of courts and their replacement by a single High Court in each of the Presidency towns, were applied in 1861; and codes of law, incorporating Indian family law almost untouched, were simultaneously published; but these changes merely summarized the work of thirty years. Over the whole range of state policy it was plain that the traditional principles of the Company were to be observed.

2. THE GROWTH OF COMMUNICATIONS

But forces more powerful than either the British or Indian Government were destined to exercise a more sweeping influence on the course of policy; and of these one of the most important was the development of quick communications, bringing India closer to world influences and multiplying the points of contact. In 1800 by sailing ship—even by the fastest and most renowned East Indiamen—it took upwards of nine months to get a reply from India; the new steamships of the middle century reduced the time to three months and, after the Suez Canal was opened in 1869, the voyage took no more than twenty-five days. By 1865 connection between London and Calcutta, by a precarious and somewhat unsatisfactory overland route it is true, was made by telegraph line, and five years later a submarine cable via the Red Sea, entirely under British control, put the home and Indian governments in direct, secure communication not thirty-six hours apart. In India itself by 1870 railways, telegraphs and postal services linked Calcutta, Lahore in the north-west, Bombay and Madras, and where the railways went there the roads ran to meet them.

3. ECONOMIC CONSEQUENCES

The economic consequences of this revolution were profound. For the first time goods and heavy crops could be moved in quantity about India and her local markets therefore gave way to Indian markets: local gluts and shortages could swiftly be met, and local prices became Indian prices. More important, advices on the state of world markets could quickly be obtained and Indian crops, especially wheat, transported in steam-driven cargo ships, found their place in international trade, with the result that Indian agricultural prices, which had always tended to be low, rose to the level of world prices with advantage to the Indian middleman though unfortunately not always to the Indian peasant. The plentiful and cheap supply of labour encouraged experiments in new crops largely through European initiative and capital. Indian tea, coffee and jute soon assumed world importance along with her raw cotton, grains, hides, oil seeds and minerals. Steadily the value of India's exports rose: in 1855 to about £23 millions, in 1900 to some £53 millions, and ten years later to £137 millions: a six-fold increase in just over half a century.

Meanwhile Britain continued to flood the Indian market with her Lancashire-made cotton cloths, and an India that was exporting more could naturally afford to buy more, including also the much-needed heavy engineering equipment for railways and bridges, which Britain's industry was well fitted to supply. India's imports therefore also rose in value, from £13½ millions in 1855 to £86 millions in 1910. It was inevitable that Britain, the strongest industrial power in the world, should dominate the trade of a dependent and primarily agricultural India: in so many ways their economies were so obviously complementary; and in fact Britain, correctly assessing the position and using her customary good commercial sense, made no effort to arrogate preferential treatment for her trade with India or to exclude foreigners from that trade. In 1870, for example, nearly a sixth of India's total trade was with countries outside the British Empire, in 1910 nearly one half.

Although these developments brought a marked increase in wealth to India, she nevertheless paid the penalty of her political subordination. Britain, partly through intellectual conviction, partly because she could manufacture and carry what the world wanted, believed in the policy of free trade, and India, although in a radically different situation, perforce accepted that policy and suffered the accompanying hardships.

Whereas Canada and Australia, in achieving self-government, claimed and gained the right to protect with tariffs their young industry and growing trade, India was exposed: her general customs tariff of 10 per cent was halved in 1875 and abolished in 1882, and although a revenue tariff of 5 per cent on imports was restored in 1894, the pressure on the cabinet of British, especially Lancashire, trading interests ensured that British cotton goods should be admitted at a 3½ per cent tariff and at the same time a countervailing excise duty of 3½ per cent be imposed on those grades of cloth produced in Indian mills which competed with those of Lancashire. This consciously applied incident of policy, in marked contrast with the general free enterprise attitude of British traders, was resisted, though in vain, even by the Governor-General and his Council, and bitterly resented throughout India. Through it Britain's material gain may have been considerable; her moral loss was certainly enormous.

Nevertheless, Indian large-scale industry began slowly to emerge. The Bengal coalfield was opened to facilitate the growth of railways, at the same time marking out the nearest large centre, Calcutta, as potentially and in fact the greatest industrial town in India. The removal in 1860 of the unfairly high duties on the import of factory machines encouraged the building of jute mills there in the sixties; and in Cawnpore, Nagpur and Madras, pioneer factories using local materials such as leather and paper, often started by Europeans and later in many instances taken up by Indians, were created. On the west coast in Bombay cotton mills were built—fifty by 1880—in the main by Parsi business men; and, at Ahmadabad, Hindu capital and enterprise created a new industrial town, now the sixth largest in India. Most of the capital for development was provided, however, by the British, for India offered the safest field in the world for their investments and trade. By 1900 nearly £200 millions of the public debt of India, largely incurred through the expensively built railways, and some £300 millions of investments in the new industries, such as jute and tea, were held by Britons. To give greater coherence to their enterprises the British extended to India their system of modern banking and of commercial law and linked Indian currency, based on the silver rupee, with the pound sterling.

Despite these industrial and commercial developments the bulk of India's peoples steadily became poorer. The vast proportion of India's wealth came from the land and necessarily the basis of her trade with Britain remained the exchange of raw materials for manufactured articles. Therefore, in the first instance, only a marked increase in her agricultural productivity could materially improve the standard of living of most of her people, but such an improvement did not take place and for a variety of reasons. In the first place, quickened by the British protective methods of rule, the Indian population rose from 206 millions in 1872, the year of the first census, to 315 millions in 1911, an increase certainly no greater in proportion than that in Western Europe or U.S.A. in the same period but, alas, not similarly accompanied by a corresponding increase in productive capacity per head. The steady, if slow, creation of new and more fertile land through irrigation by the building of canals and dams was more than offset by this increase. A steady pressure on the soil began (which still continues), finally producing a thing unknown in India before—a competitive bidding for productive land. The persistent Indian custom of dividing the land among the sons on the death of the father still further fragmented the family holdings and reduced production. Indian capital, which under a more far-seeing government might have been used to speed the rate of expansion of Indian industry, was at first brushed aside by British capital and enterprise and thus diverted into agriculture, unfortunately not for constructive experiment or at a low rate of interest, but rather in the form of a money-lending business and at a ruinous rate of interest—25 per cent being common, and 35 per cent not unknown. Peasants the world over seek relief from the routine of their life in expensively large and impressive marriage feasts and funerals, and the Indian is no exception. For those occasions he will borrow possibly the equivalent of a year's earnings, and, once accepted at high interest, this amount could never be repaid. Literally, he came into the world in debt and died in debt. At the end of the century the central government tried hard to extricate the peasants from this financial tangle, which was the more vicious in that it inhibited the planning of future crops, by exhorting them to contribute to co-operative credit societies, but the funds collected—some £6,000,000 among 31,800 societies by 1919—were too small to exercise much influence. Only a simultaneous scientific improvement in agriculture over a large part of British India could have solved a problem of this size, but the Government, for its part, expected such a development to come in the first place, as in England, from the cultivators themselves. Yet from the Indian peasant, born of a tradition and reared in a society in which one's duty was to accept rather than initiate, his vigour sapped by ill-health and an inadequate diet, it was asking too much. Indian agriculture therefore remained backward, and the peasant amidst rising prices poverty-stricken.

F

The consequences on the whole Indian economy were deep and far-reaching. Most important of all, the Government, too, remained poor: for traditionally, as we have seen, it drew the bulk of its revenues from its share in the produce of the land. Increasingly aware, as the value of land and crops rose, of the initial mistake in fixing permanently the rate of land revenue in Bengal, the Government strove to establish a system in the rest of British India which should be flexible enough to yield, both to the peasant and Government, an increasing income and at the same time stable enough to encourage long-term planning. From demanding at first one-third to one-half of the gross produce of the soil, the Government by a process of trial and error came finally to claim not more than one half—and very often much less—of the peasant's *net* return, and, although this amount seems high, no difficulty was experienced in normal years in collecting it, possibly because by modern standards other Indian taxation was low.

But unfortunately between 1866 and 1878, and again between 1897 and 1908, large parts of India were struck by famine and, in the words of one Finance Minister, the budget became only too clearly "a gamble in rain." In these circumstances a secure financial system could not be established, a reduction in the general level of taxation could not be undertaken and a steady increase in the government debt was unavoidable.

Moreover, the wisdom of the Government's distribution of expenditure is questionable. In the 1880's, for example, out of a total revenue of some £50,000,000 (50 crores) about one-third was spent on the army and one-half on the civil administration, particularly on the law courts, the police and the collection of the revenues. Strikingly small amounts remained for education and health services. Part of the heavy expenditure on the army and civil administration is accounted for by the fact that the military and civil system was English and in its higher ranks was manned by Britons, who could hardly be expected to serve in India without an adequate monetary inducement: indeed all members of what came to be called the Indian Civil Service could look forward in the course of a normal career to reaching a salary of at least £2,000 a year. The army in India was maintained at about 150,000, including

60,000 British troops, all borne on the Indian revenues, and although large forces were undoubtedly needed to safeguard internal peace and the vulnerable north-west approaches it was quite indefensible, as sometimes happened, to employ them for Imperial purposes outside India at India's expense, especially when the defence of India was not directly involved. Cases in point were the campaigns in Egypt and the Sudan (1882–1885 and 1896), in the Boer War (1899–1902) and in China (1900–1).

When one bears in mind the negligible military expenditure at this period of other British dependencies, such as Canada and Australia, it becomes evident that the forces in India were envisaged as a kind of Imperial reserve, and although she enjoyed virtually free of charge the added protection of the British Navy so also did the Empire as a whole. In plain truth, even though defence expenditure rightly held first place, a poor country like India could not properly afford to spend so much on the army and civil administration and so little on social services. Her budget may have been balanced yearly, yet her proportionate expenditure was certainly unbalanced, and her social progress slow.

4. POLITICAL CONSEQUENCES

The shrinkage of the world brought about by quicker communications transformed not only the economic life of India but also the Government's political policy, and even its jealously-guarded traditional routine. From 1864 onwards the growing railway system enabled Lord Lawrence, the Viceroy, and his staff to spend half the year at the cool summer capital of Simla in the hills, where contacts were almost exclusively official, and to return for the winter into the heart of the European industrial and commercial community in Calcutta, and succeeding Viceroys followed this practice. As a young man Lawrence had once startled the Anglo-Indian world by taking no more than fourteen days to ride from Calcutta to Delhi; but, when movement by train across India became so swift, he and his fellow Governors, and their successors, who would otherwise have made many of their journeys by horse, usually passed through without really seeing India. Thus their

Secretariats increasingly came to act as the "refractive media" through which they observed the people, and a Government already aloof became also remote from its people. In India power confined rather than corrupted the British.

Lord Lawrence was the first Viceroy to suffer the close and direct scrutiny of a Secretary of State only thirty odd hours away, which perhaps accounts for the transformation of a man of normally decisive character into a somewhat hesitant Governor-General. With the opening of a telegraph route to India in 1865, and its consolidation by submarine cable in 1870, the statutory power, which the home government had always in theory enjoyed, of controlling Indian policy, both in principle and detail, became at last effective. As Sir Charles Wood, the Secretary of State for India, explained, it led "to more references home, to more interference from home, to shrinking from responsibility in India and to meddling from home—all which things will not improve the administration."

Elgin, for example, Governor-General between 1894 and 1898, was in the habit of telegraphing London twice a day for instructions. The only possible check on the Secretary of State was simultaneously weakened, for Parliament in London, in contrast to its former practice of inquiring into the East India Company's policy, rarely troubled him with "an excessive display of affection," and through the "padded room" of the India Office the voice of India was heard less clearly than ever by the British people.

As one would expect, the Secretary of State's interference was first felt in financial matters—Morley, for instance, when in charge of the India Office, describing himself as "the ferocious dragon of the old legend watching the golden apples"—but it soon spread through all branches of government. The India Office kept the Calcutta Government under close control, perforce the Governor-General in turn closely watched the Provincial Governments who were compelled in self-defence to scrutinize carefully the work of the district officers. Indian administration, already highly centralized, was therefore still further focused on Calcutta and the always difficult task of the Viceroy became almost insupportable. Ripon, soon after his arrival in India in 1880, reported home,

"The power of the Viceroy is really terribly great—greater than I expected. Office in England is a bagatelle compared to it. Who is sufficient for such a task?" All Viceroys, even those of superhuman energy like Curzon, wilted under the united strain of overmuch work and responsibility, and an unaccustomed climate. The complaining, bitter tone of their letters home as they approached the close of their usual five-year term of office, dramatically reveals the speed of their deterioration: India killed Canning and Elgin; disrupted Dalhousie, Curzon and Minto, and broke the hearts of most of the others.

Fully occupied in their daily routine, the Viceroys and their staffs could scarcely find time and energy for long term planning, or even occasionally to survey the trend of affairs.

Taking a broad view, it was doubtless an advantage that the Central Government should be forced to think of India as a whole, that it should see the need in a country which was as large as Europe to introduce a degree of uniformity, especially by codifying the law and by pressing the most efficient methods from each province on all others. But the cries of efficiency and uniformity were repeated so frequently that they became accepted as ends in themselves, the administration seeming to forget that for Indians, like all other peoples, efficiency and single-mindedness in government could never adequately be a substitute for self-government. Curzon might declare and believe that "efficiency in administration is . . . a synonym for the contentment of the governed," but Minto's rejoinder struck the answering note in the hearts of educated Indians— "Efficiency goes too far if it carries with it a sense of injustice," and to Indians it was no consolation at all to know that in day to day administration the British Indian Government was probably the ablest and most honest the world had ever known.

The impact of the home Government was felt most strongly in foreign policy. Hitherto, the Governor-General as the man on the spot had been obliged in self-defence to take his own course, but from 1870, when the Red Sea cable was completed, Indian and British foreign policy became one, and the Governor-General in this matter found himself reduced at times to the position of an ambassador.

Foreign policy tends to be determined by national fears,

real or anticipated, and with the Russian Government still
bent on using the threat of intervention in India for effect
in European diplomacy, the British cabinet sought to maintain Afghanistan as a friendly buffer state. Consequently,
when the Russians occupied Turkestan in 1867, Sher Ali,
the ruler of Afghanistan and a nominee of the British, point-
blank asked for a British guarantee of military help, but
to this Gladstone's cabinet, which at this time held office,
would not at once agree and Sher Ali therefore turned
to Russia. But in England, Disraeli displaced Gladstone
as prime minister and in 1876 despatched Lord Lytton to
India as governor-general with orders to make British
influence supreme in Afghanistan. On his arrival Lytton
insisted that British representatives should be received at
Kabul, and, on receiving no reply, promptly ordered the
invasion of Afghanistan. Sher Ali at once fled to Russia. His
son, Yakub Khan, however, stayed behind and recognized the
fact of British supremacy, but unfortunately for himself failed
to persuade his countrymen of his right to succeed his father,
and it was a stronger personality altogether, Abdurrahman,
who, with British military help—including a wonderful forced
march by Roberts's column from Kabul to Kandahar, 313
miles in 21 days,—finally established himself as ruler and
accepted the protection of the British. After an uneasy interval
war between Russia and Britain again appeared likely in
1885 over a boundary dispute, and once again in 1902 over the
threatened independence of Tibet, but the growth of the power
of Germany in Europe brought the two governments together
in 1907, both for once seeing, what had in fact long been true,
that their strategic interests in Europe and Asia did not clash.

The mountainous tribal areas between India and Afghanistan remained restless, and despite the maintenance of large and
expensive forces along the frontiers and the incorporation in
1901 of a number of the areas in a North West Frontier
Province, armed risings and raidings continued and still
continue to take place. It is clear that the root problem is
economic and only the enrichment of the area, possibly through
the extension of fruit growing, will settle it. The other open
land frontier on the north-east was much quieter and was

further bolstered by the annexation of Upper Burma in 1885. Thus secured against attack by land and sea India's peoples, especially her "intellectuals," began to take for granted this state of affairs and even to assume that it would last indefinitely. Their confidence was rudely shaken in the Second World War.

Through every branch of government, through every facet of policy, English influences played with increasing force on India. Whereas the Company, for example, had made treaties on an equal legal footing with the Indian states, the Crown specifically claimed, as sovereign universal authority, the allegiance of the princes: stimulated by social and moral reformers in England and India it actively supervised their government, and in case of need removed them from office. Yearly, too, the Indian Government itself was called on to place before Parliament a "Material and Moral Progress Report on British India"—the title itself making explicit Britain's acceptance of those responsibilities. Great attention was given to the evolution of a famine policy, thousands of miles of railway being especially built for this purpose, and the latest technical developments in the closely allied departments of Irrigation and Forestry being applied, until it became true to say that the famine relief system was proof against any calamity except the conjunction of famine with civil or external war.

5. THE BIRTH OF INDIAN NATIONALISM

Most profound by far of all European influences were those that took effect through the spread of English education. In evolving an educational policy the most powerful groups in the Company's governments had remained consistent at least in one view, the importance of providing an education through English for a minimum number of suitable Indians. This was pursued from a variety of motives—mainly to provide a pool of cheap assistants for the civil administration, but also, on the part of some, to prepare the way for the spread of Christianity, and of others to anglicize the Indians, so increasing the demand for British manufactures ; lastly, in some degree animating all, the feeling which existed that intrinsically English education was superior to anything that India had to offer. But by 1850 the number of Indians with the required literary training in English was beginning to outstrip the Company's needs and this limited policy had already come under fire as "sending forth grandiloquent grumblers, as able to clamour as unable to work." Other critics pointed out that "if any scheme of public instruction is really to reach the Indian peoples, it must take as its basis their mother tongues," that is to say, their spoken and not their classical languages. Some asked whether any system of schooling that ignored the influence of the home by excluding women and girls could possibly have a lasting or balanced effect; and others, looking at the condition of India, appealed first for more teachers, doctors and engineers.

Perplexed between these diverse and yet comprehensive demands, the Company in 1854 approved the famous educational despatch drawn up by the President of the Board of Control, Sir Charles Wood. In effect he took the administrator's easy way out of immediate difficulties by simultaneously accepting almost all points of view and therefore imposed on the Government of India the duty of "creating a properly articulated system of education from the primary school to the University." But in accord with the ideas of the time, not only in India but in England, education remained, along with the other social services, one of the last of the charges on the Government of India's budget, and this grandiose scheme was therefore carried out "on the cheap." Had unlimited resources been available, it would have been difficult to achieve; with only scanty funds it was impossible.

In teaching as in most professions, apart from the small percentage who feel the call, the state gets what it pays for, and under the new system the quality of instruction therefore tended to remain low; the supply of textbooks was never adequate, the purchase of the relatively expensive scientific and technical equipment something to be frowned on; and the total numbers to be provided for vastly in excess of the constructive resources of the state. In these circumstances those parts of the system which were already firmly established tended to pull away from the rest. In proportion, the Government continued to spend most on the academic type of secondary and higher education, arguing that the knowledge so gained by the literate groups would soon become diffused among the mass of people. But not even in England did an academic type of higher education permeate the whole of society and still less in India did it seep among a people divided by castes in watertight compartments. To-day in India higher literary education through English still over-shadows the progress made in primary and in technical educa-tion; while female education lags even further behind. The system as a whole remains, as it started, top heavy and lop-sided. "In Bengal to-day with more undergraduates than England only one man in ten can read and write."

Nevertheless, with all its lack of balance in development, education through English has revolutionized the thought and life of India. In the Presidency capitals at first and, as time passed, in the large provincial centres also, numbers of Indians, mainly drawn from the higher literate castes of Hindu society, came directly into touch with western thought, especially through the study of English history. That the subjects of a state should be politically active instead of merely submissive, that the law should be enforced on all alike, that everyone was entitled to political rights, were profoundly new conceptions, which on the one hand provoked cultured Hindus into a new intellectual, literary and artistic activity, and on the other evoked the pertinent query, "When will such political privileges be extended to India?"

In short, over the middle decades of the nineteenth century, there sprang into being an Indian urban class, largely Hindu, undergoing the same kind of training, with interests and ideas in common, and with similar ambitions of acquiring a know-ledge of English and of entering the government service. The timely spread of the railways and postal services, and the growth of an Indian press, both in English and the vernacular, gave them a hitherto unknown class consciousness at first provincial and later national, and provided Indians with the means for the first time in their history of making an effective, united, simultaneous and countrywide response. Among these groups, and under these conditions, it was inevitable that the sentiment of Hindu nationalism should be born and nurtured. From the beginning the great majority of western-educated

Indians deliberately copied and wholeheartedly admired the British, but there always remained a strongly critical minority, drawing strength from orthodox Hinduism, who viewed English education as despoiling Indian culture, and who from time to time were reinforced by those who failed to gain the employment, especially in the government service, to which they felt their western training entitled them.

As we have seen, it was the higher caste Hindus who took quickly to English learning and ideas; the Muslims, with disastrous consequences for themselves, at first stood aside. Followers of a dogmatic, clearly defined creed which in effect constituted their whole way of life and culture, they deemed western education meaningless and therefore inferior, and their religious advisers led the way by forbidding them, under pain of eternal damnation, from acquiring the learning of the West.

Moreover, the Muslim landed aristocracy could not forget that it was they who had been displaced from the mastery of India by the British. During and after the Mutiny they naturally fell under suspicion and as a retort they took the obvious course of vaunting their own culture to prove their independence of the new Raj. Although they affected to despise the activities of Christian missionaries, the Muslims were not left entirely unmoved and, just as among the Hindus, reformers among them were provoked into preaching a revival and purification of Islam. But, significantly, whereas leading Hindu reformers, like Ram Mohun Roy and Keshab Chandra Sen, took advantage of western ideas and did not hesitate to speak and write in English, the Muslim protagonists, the most influential of whom perhaps was Ghalib, sought to achieve their renaissance through the exclusive use of Persian and Urdu, and between 1815 and 1857 in the neighbourhood of Delhi they undoubtedly achieved considerable success.

But the events of the Mutiny brought to the front, in the person of Sayyid Ahmad, a Muslim whose point of view was quite different. A nobleman, whose ancestors had held high office under the Mughals, who had himself faithfully served the East India Company, particularly distinguishing himself in the Mutiny, he spoke with authority. In his view the Muslims needed a spiritual, cultural and political regeneration which could be produced only through education on western lines. By articles and pamphlets in both Urdu and English, by a long sojourn abroad to study English life, by establishing a monthly journal, *The Reform of Morals*, by tours and speeches, by a lifetime of single-minded effort, culminating in the establishment of an Anglo-Oriental College at Aligarh (1877) to give Muslims a training on English lines, he succeeded "in arresting the degeneration of a whole people." Through him they regained confidence and developed a more constructive attitude of mind, and henceforth under western influence a new spirit of self-assertiveness among the Muslim community grew side by side with the rising consciousness of Indian middle-class unity.

But all Sayyid Ahmad's efforts could not make good the ground lost by the Muslims' comparatively late acceptance of western education: mentally and materially, as already in numbers, the Hindus had established their predominance, and nowhere was this more obvious than in the public services. In Bengal, for example, in 1871 of the 773 Indians occupying responsible government posts, the Muslims, despite their total numerical equality in the province with Hindus, held only 92 as compared with the Hindus' 681. Yet little more than a century before the Muslims, as the intellectual and political power in India, had held the monopoly of such appointments.

6. BRITISH INTENTIONS

Meanwhile the Government continued to concentrate on its day to day administration and seemingly had not carefully considered the long term effects of its general policy. At best a vague generalization was accepted, that the spread of English education would gradually permit the change from bureaucratic to more representative government in India, but no attempt whatsoever was made deliberately to guide policy towards a defined objective, or indeed to co-ordinate and make coherent the various, related branches of policy. The British Government in fact during the second half of the nineteenth century neither clarified nor made up its mind on the aim of its rule in India and the means to achieve it.

This confusion contrasts strongly with the clarity and

certainty of the Company's political policy. There was no doubt among the Company's Governors that they ruled by the force of arms and that, as Lord Hastings said in 1818, "A time not very remote will arrive when England will, on sound principles of policy, wish to relinquish the domination which she has gradually . . . assumed over this country," In 1824, in a famous passage, Sir Thomas Munro insisted, "We should look upon India, not as a temporary possession, but as one which is to be maintained permanently until the natives shall in some future age have abandoned most of their superstitions and prejudices and become sufficiently enlightened to frame a regular government for themselves, and to conduct and preserve it.

Whenever such a time shall arrive, it will probably be best for both countries that the British control should gradually be withdrawn." In 1833 Macaulay, on behalf of the British Government, declared that the day when Indians had acquired this capacity to govern themselves like Englishmen through representative institutions would be "the proudest day in English history." Many others testified to the same effect, but the Whig conception of representative government in those days was far short of modern democracy and it was taken for granted that responsibility *would be handed to a rejuvenated Indian royal and aristocratic class* whose powers and privileges thereafter might gradually be limited as had happened in England.

But by the 1870's the position had changed completely. The Mutiny had profoundly shocked British opinion, and British rulers no longer lightly spoke of relinquishing an India which had just been reconquered after a desperate struggle. Moreover, the Muslim aristocracy in northern India was regarded with the gravest suspicion for the part, real or fancied, which they had played in the Mutiny, and for their reluctance to be "improved" by the West, a clear demonstration in British eyes of their irresponsibility. Whereas Munro had been writing at a time when it was still fashionable to think of colonies as millstones round the mother country's neck—(indeed in that same year, 1824, the Foreign Secretary, George Canning, had urged that the British should hand over Singapore to the Dutch!)—the Viceroys were borne up by a rising British feeling of pride in the Empire, perhaps best expressed in Disraeli's presentation to Queen Victoria in 1877 of the title of "Empress of India." Disraeli could not have said more clearly that the British Raj was there to stay, and, if further justification was needed, the fact and fear of expanding Russian power in Asia could be pointed to. Behind him both within and outside Parliament stood the British commercial interests who knew they had found in India the safest field of investment and trade in the world.

Against this background the Government in India could hardly be expected to view with unmitigated satisfaction the growth of an Indian middle class intelligentsia whose chief public interests inevitably lay in politics and in the possibility of achieving a more representative form of government. Indeed, the more the British studied the matter, the more aware they became not of this possibility, but rather of the difficulties arising through Indian dissimilarities in custom, race and religion.

In 1881 Sir Auckland Colvin, Lieutenant-Governor of the North West Provinces and one of the most enlightened of British officials, could write, "No nation, least of all a nation in the East, can be trusted within less than a lifetime of a living man, to adopt and put into practice conceptions of political life confined at present mainly to the Anglo-Saxon race." Unable in any event to see where such a policy might lead, yet at the same time unable to deny the whole trend of the British liberal tradition in parliamentary history, the Government became confused in mind on the proper constitutional policy to be pursued, meanwhile concealing this under a cautious and cool attitude to all politically-minded Indians.

We can clearly perceive this confusion of thought if we examine the various aspects of the Government's domestic policy over the later part of the nineteenth century. Particularly, the courses of its policies towards the press, towards the admission of Indians to the higher ranks of the public service, towards the development of representative government, not only ran contrary to its educational plans but also at cross purposes with one another. In consequence the substitution of popular for despotic rule—a delicate transition in the most favourable circumstances—proceeded through such exaggerated turmoil, suffering and frustration that Indian politics became almost a synonym for deadlock.

7. THE INDIAN PRESS

The Government's attitude towards the press was calculated to exasperate by giving Indians the greatest scope to develop their complaints without at the same time affording remedies. Through the spread of education the press had grown rapidly in size: in 1877 in Indian languages alone, for instance, there were sixty-two such papers in the Bombay Presidency, about the same number in northern India, some twenty-eight in Bengal and about a score in southern India, and their total circulation reached the neighbourhood of 100,000. Newspapers in English found an even wider public.

Because the idea of a free press was accepted in England, the East India Company had set free the press in India and, despite the marked difference between the governments of the two countries, the Crown persisted in this policy. But, whereas in England, the proper exercise of the undoubted powers of a free press could and did promote better government, in India the central authority was not open to like influence and an uncensored press therefore formed an anomaly.

Through their awareness of their ineffective, indeed irresponsible, function, the Indian newspapers on political matters usually took a bitterly hostile and contemptuous attitude, including at times even incitements to assassination. In 1878 it was felt advisable to pass a Vernacular Press Act bringing the wildest groups under some degree of control, but within four years the Act, which had provoked resentment in India and opposition in England, was repealed by Governor-General Ripon. In the following year, 1883, a violent press storm arose over the objection of the English tea and indigo planters in Bengal to a quite proper Government proposal—the Ilbert Bill—to give senior Indian magistrates in the Civil Service power to try Englishmen. A large section of the indigenous press waxed wrath at this implied sense of superiority and a press campaign was fought on racial grounds, the European community obviously being inspired by a false notion of their position in India. Indeed as Thomas Munro, one of the wisest Englishmen who served in India, had long since declared, the first duty of a free press would undoubtedly be to rid India of her foreign yoke.

In fact, starting in 1858, it would not have been difficult to have devised a more coherent and less aggravating press policy for, during the Mutiny, the excesses of the newspapers on both sides had forced the Government to impose a strict censorship, and thereafter an easy and desirable course would probably have been to release control over the newspapers step by step with the growth of educated public opinion and of representative government. As it was, largely because of an unthinking application of English ideas, the press policy actually chosen was the most trouble-making for Government and people alike.

8. HIGHER EMPLOYMENT FOR INDIANS

Logically enough, when Cornwallis introduced an English system of administration into the Company's possessions, the higher posts in it were at the same time reserved for Europeans, and despite protests by Munro and others that the undoubted advantages of such a system were "purchased by the sacrifice of independence of national character, and of whatever renders a people respectable," this practice was consistently applied by the Company. Although in 1858 Queen Victoria proclaimed that "Our subjects, of whatever race and creed, be freely and impartially admitted to offices in Our service, the duties of which they may be qualified by their education, ability and integrity to perform," the same policy in effect was maintained.

Meanwhile in 1853, replacing the custom of appointment by nomination, an open competitive examination in London had been established through which the higher posts in the Indian Civil Service were to be filled. In theory, it was true, Indians could compete but faced by an examination base on English courses, coupled with an expensive and lengthy sea voyage that by Hindu social rule would automatically outcaste any Hindu making it, few took the risk. In 1863 a Bengali,

Satyendra Nath Tagore, dared and succeeded: six years later three more Bengalis followed him. But although more Indians began to travel to London, Government policy steadily made their task almost impossible, for the maximum age of entry, which had been twenty-three in 1853, was progressively lowered until in 1878 it stood at nineteen; which in effect reserved for Britons the very great majority of these competitive posts.

The line of argument used by George Otto Trevelyan, himself a member of the Indian Civil Service, in urging this policy is worth quoting for the point of view it reveals: "By choosing your civilians at an earlier age you will get hold of a class who now slip through your hands. A man of first-rate powers who has once tasted the sweets of University success will never be persuaded to give up his English hopes. At two and twenty, in the full view of a Trinity or Merton fellowship, who would consent to exchange the Common Room in being, and Downing Street in prospect for the bungalow and the cutcherry? Warren Hastings and Sir Charles Metcalfe were among the best scholars of their time at Eton and Westminster. If they had once worn the gown they would have been lost for ever to India. Put the limit of age some three years earlier and you will have a fair chance of getting a Metcalfe every other year and a Hastings once in a decade."

Unfortunately for this argument, the India in which Warren Hastings and Metcalfe could exercise their talents to the full had long disappeared, and, properly viewed, the relevant problem was rather the admission to the public service not of Englishmen but of Indians. Already, disturbed by the obvious contradiction between an educational policy which was turning out hundreds of University graduates and a Civil Service policy that virtually excluded Indians from all higher posts, the Government in 1879 turned on its tracks and decided to establish a new "statutory civil service" by setting aside twenty per cent of its higher posts "for young men of good family and social position, possessed of fair abilities and education to whom the offices which were open to them . . . had not proved sufficient inducement to them to come forward." This policy sought to recruit from the old aristocracy, not from the new middle-class intelligentsia, but standards had so far changed and the aristocracy so far degenerated that sufficient numbers of the desired type were not forthcoming. By 1886 only seven of the twenty per cent of posts set aside for them had been filled and it was therefore decided in that year to abandon this scheme and return to a more liberal interpretation of the former policy. Accordingly, the maximum age for taking the London examination was raised first to twenty-three, and in 1906 to twenty-four, though all proposals, including a resolution of the House of Commons in 1893, to introduce simultaneous examinations in India and England were resisted until after the First World War: and at the time of its outbreak in 1914 over eighty per cent of the highest posts still remained in British hands.

A public service policy consistent with the Government's established educational plan for producing hundreds of Indian graduates would have included as early as the 1860's or 1870's the grant of a limited number of scholarships to England and at the same time measures facilitating promotion from the lower ranks of the service. Then, after the Indian educational system itself had gained the necessary sound footing, simultaneous examinations in India and England could have been introduced. Some immediate loss of efficiency in administration might indeed have followed, but the gain in Indian satisfaction would have been great.

As it was, the most enterprising of the western-educated Indians tended to seek careers in law and journalism, two spheres in which distinction, position and wealth lay open to Indians of moderate means. From the time of Cornwallis the law courts had offered not only a lucrative but also a most congenial profession, especially to the higher and literate castes, among whom a retentive memory and a feeling for word play had always been prized. So notable, indeed, was their contribution that in 1861 the highest judicial posts in India were opened to them, and henceforth few able Indians chose to enter the lower ranks of the public service or of medicine or teaching or engineering, where pay was small and prospects doubtful, when they could embark on a legal career. Journalism, too, yielded similar rewards, and thus among the rising intelligentsia there stood forth a class of journalists and lawyers,

G

bound together by common interests, imbued with the independent spirit of the English press and the English Bar and enjoying a mastery of the spoken and written word. Peculiarly fitted to wage a political campaign, they did not miss an opportunity of introducing politics into India.

9. THE BEGINNINGS OF REPRESENTATIVE GOVERNMENT

The shock of the Mutiny drove both the London and the Calcutta Governments to consider how to achieve a closer contact with Indian opinion in order to avoid a similar tragedy in future. Sayyid Ahmad, the loyal and enterprising Muslim champion, urged that the best way would be for the Governor-General to nominate Indian non-official representatives to sit on his Council, and in 1861 Lord Canning adopted this point of view with the very important proviso that these new members were to join the Council only for legislative purposes: discussion and criticism of the executive, even the right to ask questions, were prohibited. It is quite clear that, in establishing this Legislative Council, Canning was not following English parliamentary precedents, but rather the practice of Indian princes, who traditionally at their *durbar*, or audience, sought the opinion of their subjects, so to prevent minor grievances growing into major storms. Canning's viewpoint was well summed up by Sir Bartle Frere, Governor of Bombay, "Unless you have some barometer or safety valve in the shape of a deliberative council, I believe you will always be liable to very unlooked for and dangerous explosions."

But western-educated Indians rejected this point of view: as Macaulay had hoped, they had become English in ideas and culture, and for them, brought up on the works of Burke and Mill and impressed by the constructive force of English liberalism, parliamentary government after the British fashion stood as the ideal. Arguing that Britain the world over always supported nationalism and the spread of British democratic forms of government, they saw India as a nation in prospect and themselves as the proper constitutional channel through which parliamentary practices could be introduced.

The various and important implications of this assumption seem not at this time to have been fully considered or understood either in England or India.

English parliamentary practices rested upon the possibility of government through a comparatively well-educated public, living in circumstances which allowed the quick evolution of responsible public opinion. The British people themselves were homogeneous enough for all to discuss and vote together more or less amicably; and to abide by majority decisions; and for all local governments to work harmoniously under one national legislature, flexibility in that body being achieved through a two-party system. But Indian society was not homogeneous; neither was it compact nor educated enough quickly to evolve a public opinion: moreover, it was so split as to make majority decisions unpopular and unworkable. To determine that some form of constitutional government in India was both desirable and practicable in the course of time was praiseworthy, but to strive to apply the *English* parliamentary system in India was to attempt the impossible.

On the assumption that with British help all was possible these fundamental considerations were quite obscured for Indians by the excitement of day to day agitation. A mere advisory place in the country's administration in the persons of Government nominees was soon felt to be inadequate, and through persistent demands in the press the Government was induced to extend the sphere in which Indians could influence the Government. It took a characteristically English form.

In Britain the central government had sprung from and always relied on the strength of local government, and, between 1873 and 1883, to Mayo and Ripon, the two Governors-General chiefly concerned, it seemed proper, in extending the part Indians were to play in public life, to begin by providing an education in practical politics through local government. Starting with the justifiable assumption that as far as possible use should be made of indigenous institutions, they soon found that Indian local agencies were too weak and too few to achieve their purpose, and, almost despite themselves, were driven to establishing urban councils and rural boards after the English pattern, and at the same time, although they had not at first so intended, implicitly accepting the representative principle and in many cases even direct election. Even so, few able Indians could be persuaded to give freely of their time to local affairs under an alien government, and those who did soon resented the fact that no financial responsibility devolved on them; and the main burden of local work was soon resumed by the existing district officers.

10. THE INDIAN NATIONAL CONGRESS

It was evident that politically-minded Indians were seeking a more prominent stage and, finding even the press too provincial in outlook to constitute a national forum, they set about creating one. Bengalis, who had first and most steadily felt the impact of English influences, gave the lead and at Calcutta an Indian Association summoned a national conference in 1883 and again in 1885, and at the same time, on the other side of India, the now famous Indian National Congress held its first meeting at Bombay. Much of the credit for its foundation goes to an Englishman, Allan Octavian Hume, himself a retired Indian civilian and the son of a family with a long tradition of service in India.

After his retirement in 1882 Hume gave all his time and boundless energy to developing political discussion among Indians, soon concluding, in his own words, that it was "of paramount importance to find an overt and constitutional channel for the discharge of the increasing ferment which had resulted from western ideas and education." With the bluntness of speech inherited from his father, Joseph, the famous Radical member of parliament, he did not hesitate to reveal his mind to educated Indians: "Every nation secures precisely as good a government as it merits. If you, the picked men, the most highly educated of the nation, cannot, scorning personal ease and selfish objects, make a resolute struggle to secure . . . a larger share in the management of your own affairs, then we, your friends, are wrong and our adversaries right . . . Only, if this be so, let us hear no more factious, peevish complaints that you are kept in leading strings and treated like children, for you will have proved yourselves such. Men know how to act."

Along with Sir William Wedderburn, also a retired civilian

and an influential M.P., and Robert Knight, owner-editor of the *Statesman* newspaper, and a group of leading Indians Hume planned a National Congress. He first discussed the idea with the Governor-General, Dufferin, who urged that attention should be paid to political rather than social matters and gave his blessing to the project; and to the first invitation seventy-two volunteers from all parts of India responded. For this first session, which was clearly intended as an experiment, Hume's aim was stated to be simply to enable fellow workers in the political field to get to know each other so that they might create not so much a political party as "the germ of a native parliament."

From 1885 the Congress continued to meet yearly, each time at a different Indian centre, and over the first ten years, although its numbers increased, in both composition and function it tended to conform to a clear pattern.

Essentially it was a middle-class Hindu and Brahman gathering from the principal cities, the aristocratic land-owning groups from the countryside being poorly represented, and the mass of the people quite unconcerned; and it fairly represented the new middle classes, lawyers and journalists forming the most prominent group. The Brahman pre-eminence (still a mark of Congress to-day) was illustrated by their sharing the chief executive offices with Englishmen such as Hume, Wedderburn and George Yule. The Muslim members in these early years averaged less than fifteen per cent of the total and, significantly, unlike the western-educated Hindus, they were largely drawn from the landowning classes.

In the early years of the life of the Congress its annual meeting usually began with an affirmation of loyalty to Britain and an insistence on its constitutional procedure, and closed with cheers for the Queen Empress and the Viceroy. Their proposals carried yearly were moderate and conservative, in particular asking that up to one-half of the Viceroy's Legislative Council should be elected and that they should enjoy the right to discuss the budget and put questions, and secondly that simultaneous examinations in England and India for the Indian Civil Service should be instituted.

In 1892, largely on the initiative of Governor-General

Dufferin, the British Government agreed by Act of Parliament to increase the representation of Indians on the Central and Provincial Legislative Councils and to allow discussion of the budget and the asking of questions about day to day affairs. In the Government's view there was nothing revolutionary in these changes, indeed they were intended merely to extend the idea accepted in the Act of 1861. Quite simply, Indians were to be given further opportunities of advising the Governor-General, but in practice it was accepted that the most convenient way of finding the proper Indian members would be to allow local government boards and also universities, chambers of commerce and landholders' associations to put forward names for the Governor-General's consideration.

Conventionally, among these bodies the names were arrived at through election, and conventionally the Governor-General and Governors habitually accepted them, so that in a typically unobtrusive British fashion the principles of election and representation, already recognized in the sphere of local government, came also to be accepted in the Provincial and Central Legislatures. But it was representation of and election through *special* interests and not, as in Britain, through the whole body of voters in territorial constituencies, and the Government both in England and India insisted again and again that in no sense could this step be considered as "an approach . . . to English parliamentary government and an English constitution," and to underline this the Central and Provincial Government Councils still carried a majority of officials as if to emphasize the fact that the Governors enjoyed the right of veto.

11. HINDU AND MUSLIM NATIONALISM

The Indian National Congress at its meeting in 1892 at Allahabad "accepted in a loyal spirit" the Act of that year, but urged that the nomination of members through local boards hardly constituted representation of the general population. The Government, however, largely because of the increasingly hostile tone of Congress propaganda throughout British India, was no longer disposed to listen. From benignly approving it

became distinctly cool; pointing out that Congress itself was
not only unrepresentative of India but unreal in its political
thought because it consistently ignored the fundamental fact
that the government and defence of India rested on the maintenance of a strong British army and navy.

From two other quarters at the same time criticism of the
Congress arose. Inevitably, as the years had passed, some of the
younger Congressmen began to doubt whether a purely
constitutional agitation would yield the desired political results
within a measurable period of time, and this practical point of
view was especially acceptable to those who, through western
education, had found nothing but disappointment. Unfortunately, they were many, for the Government foolishly had brought
about a vast expansion in the numbers attending university
colleges without sufficiently considering beforehand whether the
students were fitted for this training and, equally important,
whether suitable, subsequent employment would be available.

In fact, on the one hand the wastage was appalling, only
one student in nine achieving his degree, and on the other
hand the only large "industry" created by the Government,
namely, the public service, virtually reserved the great bulk of
its highest posts for Europeans. To these economically and
politically disappointed young Indians the Government's
apparent acceptance of "the inevitability of gradualness" was
exasperating. They soon underwent a natural revulsion against
the "mimic Anglicism" which had availed them nought; and a
coincident revival in orthodox Hinduism provided an alternative, much more attractive source of inspiration.

The early groups of western-educated Indians had
accepted things and ideas English with enthusiasm, tending if
anything to become more English than the English themselves;
and even Ram Mohun Roy's reforming Brahmo Samaj had
deliberately attempted to fuse the best of Indian and of western
ideas and practices, but the most conservative and orthodox
Hindus had never become reconciled to western ideas.
Towards the end of the century a Hindu religious revival took
place. Through two main reforming groups, the Arya Samaj
(1875) and the Ramakrishna Mission (1879), preachers like
Dayanand and Swami Vivekananda, with the constant cry,

"Let us once again be ourselves," caught the ear of a wide circle of Hindus. Arguing that compromise was impossible with an "England whose war-flag is the factory chimney, whose troops are the merchantmen, whose battlefields are the market places of the world, and whose Empress is the shining goddess Fortune," they sought salvation through the complete rejection of the West.

To the young, frustrated Hindus this doctrine was both timely and exciting: on the one side it afforded the strongest possible religious sanction for their political and economic grievances, on the other it enabled them to abandon the customary appeal to the doctrines of Burke and Mill and instead to turn directly to Hinduism. It was accepted that in this cause all methods were justifiable in achieving the desired end, namely, the expulsion of alien influence and the political and spiritual resurrection of Hinduism. As one of their leaders wrote, "If thieves enter our house and we have not sufficient strength to drive them out we should without hesitation shut them up and burn them alive. . . . We may kill even our teachers and kinsmen and no blame attaches if we are not actuated by selfish desires."

Signs of the emergence of these extremist groups appeared in Calcutta and Poona in 1891 when the Government, which was making an attempt to prohibit the consummation of Indian marriages before the child-wife reached twelve years old, was accused of attacking Hinduism. And they appeared again in 1897 when the Government, in stamping out a plague epidemic in Western India, roused great resentment by using troops to search Poona for infected persons. The protagonist in both these agitations was a member of the justly famous Chitpavan Brahman caste named Bal Gangadhar Tilak, a man of great vigour and ability, who was convinced that India's ills were caused by foreign invaders, whether British or Muslim. He extolled Sivaji—the man of action, the Maratha leader and Hindu scourge of the Muslims—as the national hero, and both in the Congress and in his Marathi newspaper, the *Kesari*, he raged against the Government, at the same time pouring scorn on Congress's timid policy of "pray, petition and protest." He deliberately incited his audience to violence, with the result that two youths of his own caste assassinated two

English officers. Tilak was promptly tried and imprisoned, but the habit of political murder and of terrorist activity began to spread, particularly in Bengal where the middle-classes were hard hit by rising prices and the number of unemployed graduates was excessive. The advent in 1899, in the person of Curzon, of a Governor-General with the capacity and inclination but not the opportunity to be a Wellesley, who seemed to despise the Bengali intellectuals in particular, brought matters to a head. When in 1905 he sought for administrative convenience to partition the province, whose population as he said had grown from sixty-six to seventy-eight millions in thirty years, he was accused of making a veiled attack on Bengali nationalism and a provincial-wide protest arose. Curzon dismissed it—"Not . . . one single line of argument, . . . nothing but rhetoric," but popular sentiment threw up a song, *Bande Mataram*—"Hail Motherland," which has since exerted a national appeal as strong as the *Marseillaise:*

"My Motherland I sing, Thou art my head,
Thou art my heart,
My life and soul art Thou, my soul, my worship
And my Art. Before Thy feet I bow."

In the Congress the extremists made a serious effort between 1905 and 1907 to gain control and to change it from a constitutional into a revolutionary organization, but failed largely because of the outstanding character and ability of the leader of the moderates, Gopal Krishna Gokhale, a member of the same Brahman caste as Tilak, and one of the few Indians who had learnt his politics in the hard school of local government. A man who could hold his tongue, he seemed fitted to hold the highest office. In 1908 under his guidance the Congress in adopting a new constitution reaffirmed its decision to use "constitutional means by bringing about a steady reform of the existing system of administration." But this split in the National Congress was real and the more serious because on another side also it had been attacked and weakened.

Tilak's extremist agitation extolling Hindu and Maratha revivalism had been in effect not only anti-British but also anti-Muslim; and had exacerbated the already strained relations between the Congress and the Muslims. From its inception the leading Muslims had looked with disfavour on the Congress, and in 1886 prominent Muslim associations in Calcutta and Madras refused invitations to send delegates, and even among the Muslim delegates who attended severe criticism of Congress policy was voiced. Two years later the most influential of all Indian Muslims, Sir Sayyid Ahmad, created a Muslim Patriotic Association to focus Muslim opposition, using the Allahabad newspaper, the *Pioneer*, as his mouthpiece.

He outlined the Muslim viewpoint in a series of outspoken articles and speeches. India, he declared in words that have since been echoed by Mr. Jinnah, is two nations not one, and "it is our nation which conquered with its sword the whole of India." The Congress movement he defined as "a civil war without arms," and if, he went on, India were to be given, as Congress desired, an elective system based on wealth or education or numbers, "the whole Council will consist of Babu So and So"; and yet all Muslims, he said, despised "these fish-eating Babus of Bengal." Simultaneous competitive examinations for the Civil Service would not in any event benefit the backward Muslims but, if they were to be introduced, he prayed that "we be allowed to use the *pen* of our ancestors." Their clear policy, he maintained, was to boycott the Congress and to support the British.

Although one eminent Muslim, Budrudin Tyabji, opposed this attitude and favoured Hindu-Muslim co-operation within the Congress, the overwhelming majority of influential Muslims followed Sir Sayyid and therefore from the beginning the Congress's claim to be representative of India could not in fact be substantiated. Sir Sayyid's policy was frankly based on fear: fear of permanent domination—educationally, economically, politically—of Muslims by Hindus. He himself favoured a system by which Hindu and Muslim opinion would be represented on the Government's Legislative Councils, but not by election after the English fashion, and, as a former member of the Governor-General's own Legislative Council, he took every opportunity of making this point, and adding that in the working of the Indian Councils Act of 1892 the Muslims were already persistently under-represented. Although Sir Sayyid died in

1898 his followers went on in 1906 to form the All India Muslim League to defend their interests and keep their point of view before the Government.

12. THE BRITISH RESPONSE

By 1907 the spread of terrorism in Bengal and western India, and the increasing criticism of the Congress's moderate policy by the revolutionary groups, convinced Lord Minto and Lord Morley, the Governor-General and the Secretary of State, that unless action were taken quickly the Congress constitutional party under Gokhale would be completely undermined. The new Liberal cabinet in London favoured reform and agreed that Indian political grievances were substantial and that most of them were just and ought to be remedied, but, lacking a clearly distinguishable and steadily developing British policy towards the growth of politics in India, Morley and Minto were driven to devising not so much a coherent plan as a series of expedients to meet the particular and admittedly difficult situation.

Minto first demanded of Morley and succeeded in gaining considerable powers with which to fight the terrorists, and by freely using them brought the movement under control. To encourage the "moderates" the Government then recognized their long-standing demand for the opening to Indians of the highest posts by admitting Indian members directly to the Secretary of State's Council in London and one eminent Indian lawyer, later elevated as Lord Sinha, to the Governor-General's own executive council; and the Presidency councils were similarly enlarged.

But the Congress's chief and most persistent demands had been for the increase of Indian representation on the Legislative Councils and the extension of the elective principle. But the implication, in the face of the growth of Hindu extremism and of Hindu-Muslim antagonism, that this might lead to constitutional government of the English type daunted even Morley. Nevertheless, to meet the situation,—and arguing that the problem was essentially that of giving Indians greater opportunities of advising, but definitely not of controlling, the

Government,—both he and Minto agreed to allow the Legislative Councils to discuss and pass resolutions on all matters, including the budget, at the same time enlarging all the Councils and, while retaining an official majority at the centre, to concede non-official majorities in the provincial legislatures. Lastly, and most important, they recognized the principle of election to these Councils, but in the teeth of Muslim opposition they shrank from creating territorial constituencies of the British type and therefore determined to extend the system introduced in 1892 of representation by special interests.

At this stage a Muslim delegation under the Aga Khan restated the Muslims' case so forcibly to Minto, pointing out that even under the 1892 scheme they were under-represented by one-half in proportion to their numbers, that the Government decided, despite Hindu protests, to concede to Muslims, and to them alone, separate electorates in which the elections to seats reserved for them should be made by Muslims alone. In effect, the number of Muslim members was to be based on the importance rather than on the size of their community.

It was clear that under this provision Muslim electors would tend to think as Muslims rather than as Indians and would thus become more aware than ever of their own distinctiveness, and the charge has often been made that the British deliberately applied such a "divide and rule" policy. Morley and Minto, indeed, were not unaware of the possible advantages of this course, but there is no evidence to suggest that they consciously sought it. Had they set themselves to introduce parliamentary government of the English kind into India, then their recognition of separate electorates would have been a mischievous act, but they clearly had no such intention in mind.

"A sop to impossible ambitions," was Minto's description of the reforms, and Morley, in Parliament and in private, maintained that he did not "think it desirable or possible, or even conceivable, to adapt English political institutions to the nations who inhabit India." Indeed it was the march of events— the rise of the Indian middle classes, the falling behind of Muslims on the road to power, place and wealth and their consequent tendency to invoke the whole strength of their community, rich and poor, educated and ignorant, to redress the balance—that produced this modern form of communalism. Essentially, modern Indian communalism emerges as a middle-class problem and its chief causes arise through political and economic as much as through religious rivalry.

The Morley-Minto reforms of 1909 marked the close of the first phase of Indian politics. Like their predecessors in 1873, 1883 and 1892, whilst taking steps that led towards English parliamentary government in India they yet had made up their minds that it was impossible of achievement. But, seemingly, at the same time they did not decide, as was their clear duty, what were the alternatives and what steps at a later stage it would be desirable and practicable to take. Indeed, one of Morley's own afterthoughts laid bare the heart of the matter: "We ought to have thought before we tried occidental education: we applied that and occidental machinery must follow." This indeed was the view of Gokhale and the "moderates," the strongest party in India at the time, and had Morley and Minto acted on it they would have been able to try the experiment in the most favourable circumstances. But the opportunity was missed and when the attempt was made in 1919 it came too late.

.   .   .   .   .

Thus down to 1909, lacking clarity of mind and directness in approach, the British Government in India followed a confused, uncertain policy towards Indian nationalism, most of the time assuming an attitude of coolness and inflexibility —which really concealed its perplexity—varied on occasion by a retreat from position to position, each move being made a little too late to satisfy the bulk of educated Indian opinion. Just as the East India Company had overrun India whilst condemning schemes of conquest, so also the British Government took Indians towards a kind of parliamentary government whilst disavowing the possibility.

CHAPTER V

THE STRUGGLE FOR INDEPENDENCE, 1909-1946

I. INDIA COMES OF AGE

M ORLEY and Minto undoubtedly missed the best opportunity of introducing the English parliamentary system into India. Never again did more favourable conditions obtain: the Indian National Congress, the strongest party in the country, eagerly desired to co-operate with the British and, in the person of Gokhale, possessed a leader who would have been equal to his responsibilities. Yet at the same time the reforms of 1909 did give encouragement to the view that Indian responsible government could be achieved through constitutional agitation.

Most Congressmen felt that, through their Westminster Parliamentary Committee and other propaganda organizations which they had set up in England, and through the visit, for example, of Gokhale himself to put their case directly before the British Cabinet, Indian aspirations were beginning to be precisely appreciated in London. This was clearly reflected in 1914 when, on the outbreak of the First World War, most sections of Indian opinion hastened to promise their full support to Britain "in the fight for democracy and civilization." During the war India rapidly grew up, becoming, in the course of the race to out-produce Germany, not only one of the leading industrial powers in the world but the possessor of the largest volunteer army in the British Commonwealth. In effect she quickly rose to the status of a world power, internationally respected and rightfully enjoying, through her own efforts on behalf of the Allies, representation on Imperial and War Conferences and at the Versailles Treaty discussions.

Within India, however, after the first flush of enthusiasm for the war, the politicians began to contrast unfavourably their own small voice in Indian government with the evident importance of India's position in the Commonwealth.

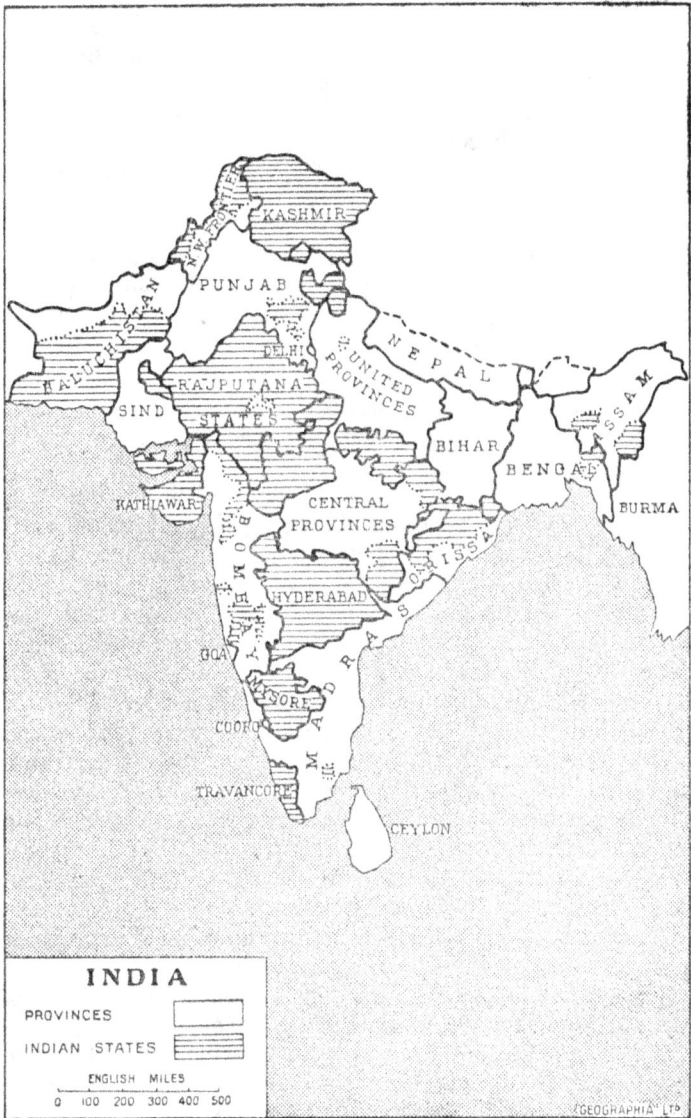

Moreover, closer acquaintance with the working of the Morley-Minto constitution had disappointed even the "moderates" in Congress. The British Government, whose representatives publicly disavowed Dominion status as India's goal, clearly did not think the Morley-Minto reforms would lead to responsible government, and Sir S. P. (afterwards Lord) Sinha, President of the Congress in 1915 and soon to be the first Indian Governor of a province, admitted the obvious when he said that the reforms led India into a political *cul-de-sac*. The consequent weakening of the position of the "moderates" combined with the death of their leader, Gokhale, in 1915, directly encouraged the more extreme elements, who reappeared in strength in the Congress of 1916; and in India generally the dislocations and disappointments of war gave increasing scope to the terrorists, particularly in Bengal. Coincidentally, the events of the war stimulated Muslim opposition to the British.

Ever since 1909 the Muslim aristocracy and middle classes had remained content in the belief that the British grant of separate electorates had guaranteed their political future *vis-à-vis* the Hindus, and they had given strong support to the war effort. But the world of Islam, like a drum which when tapped anywhere reverberates over its whole surface, grew uneasy when Britain became involved in war with the Sultan of Turkey, and Indian Muslims, who since the fall of the Mughal Empire had been in the habit of regarding him as their Caliph or spiritual head, deplored the imprudent use by the British of Muslim troops against the Turks in Mesopotamia and the obvious threat to dismember Turkey. This provocation was sufficient to bring together for the first time to consider their political future, the leaders of the Muslim League and of the predominantly Hindu Congress.

In the generous warmth of this meeting, held at Lucknow in 1916, both sides made concessions: the Congress abandoned its opposition to the Muslims' right throughout British India to separate electorates, and the Muslims, overcoming the fears of Hindu domination raised by Sir Sayyid Ahmad, accepted the Congress objectives of parliamentary government and Dominion status. With enthusiasm the President of the Muslim

League, Mr. Muhammad Ali Jinnah, an eminent Bombay lawyer, acclaimed this "Lucknow Pact" as leading to "a new India."

2. THE REVERSAL OF BRITISH POLICY

Lord Chelmsford, who assumed the Viceroyalty at this juncture, sensing the spirit of the times, especially the deep-seated feeling of political frustration, which was finding increased expression in terrorism, quickly defined his own objective for India as self-government within the Empire, whilst also turning to London for further guidance. In England, where India's war effort had impressed the mind and touched the heart of the people, the new Liberal Secretary of State for India, Edwin Montagu, felt keenly the implications for India of waging a world war "for national self-determination"; and this coincidence of a strong British sense of obligation with the renewed demands of Indians evoked in August 1917 a fresh and positive statement of British intentions in India. Montagu announced that "the policy of His Majesty's Government . . . is that of the increasing association of Indians in every branch of the administration and the gradual development of self-governing institutions with a view to the progressive realization of responsible government in India as an integral part of the British Empire."

The British change-round was complete: henceforth Indians were to be treated as a nation for whom parliamentary government of the English kind was deemed possible and therefore promised, with Dominion status to follow as a matter of course: and Montagu promptly joined Chelmsford in India to devise the constitutional means to these ends. Their proposals were summed up in a report to which life was given in the Government of India Act of 1919.

The first aim, responsible government, was to be achieved by remodelling the central and nine provincial governments of British India. Although the Viceroy necessarily remained responsible to the Secretary of State and Parliament, and therefore in all important matters retained the power to get his own way, he was given a Central Legislature consisting of an

H

Assembly and a Council of State, both with a majority of elected members, which were to debate all matters and form the germ of an Indian parliament. Side by side, a Chamber of Princes was constituted, as a purely consultative body, which was to put the point of view of the Indian States and which in time, it was hoped, would join in creating an All-India Union.

The changes in provincial government, which formed the essence of the scheme, went further by trying to bring about some degree of ministerial responsibility. The Governor of each province was to be assisted by a group of Indian ministers chosen by him from the provincial legislature; and under him the departments of state were divided in two groups, those like law and order, revenue and finance which he "reserved" under the control of his own officials, and on the other hand those like education, local government, public health and economic development which he "transferred" to Indian Ministers, who were responsible for them to the legislature. In time it was hoped that all departments might be "transferred" to Ministers and the provincial governments thus become wholly responsible. The franchise for both central and provincial legislatures was extended to about seven million voters, including 315,000 women, divided into the already accepted three classes of constituencies—local, communal and special—through which all the important interests of the diverse Indian population were to be represented.

The plan had its merits. It represented the British Government's first clear-cut decision since 1885 on the future of Indian political life. Without confusion of thought the goal was now defined: the difficulties in the way, especially the heterogeneous and ignorant population, the undemocratic Hindu caste system, the existence of separate Muslim and Sikh electorates, were not overlooked. Certainly they were minimized and, although the most ingenious scheme had been devised gradually to overcome them, the new policy as a whole was avowedly an act of faith; faith that the ignorant would be educated, faith that the communal and caste divisions would disappear, faith that English democratic institutions could nourish in India democratic ways of thought and life, faith that India could become one nation.

"The vision," the authors of the plan declared, "is one which may well lift men up to resolve on things that seemed impossible before. Is it too much to hope that the desire of the people of India so to govern themselves and the conviction that they can never do so otherwise, in any real sense, may prove eventually to be the solvent of these difficulties of race and creed?"

3. THE WORKING OF THE ACT OF 1919

This policy was first given a clear trial of ten years, and then persisted in until 1937, and it might well have succeeded had not the spirit of the times run so strongly against it from the start. It was a major misfortune that English educated opinion on India had developed so slowly because, if this plan was worth trying in 1919, it would have been equally worth trying ten years earlier when it would have been welcomed by all the more important sections of Indian political opinion. By 1919, however, that opinion had perceptibly changed. The reaction "from the exertion, the fears, and the sufferings of the past five years" was at its height: through the wartime rise in prices and poor harvests, economic distress was widespread. The Muslims felt embittered by continued British antagonism to Turkey, and the more militant among them formed a Khilafat (Caliphate) party to work for the restoration of the defeated Sultan.

In Congress the "moderates," who still stood for "constitutional gradualness," were outnumbered by the more extreme groups, among whom a new member, Mohandas Karamchand Gandhi, was beginning to exert wide influence; and from this time onwards he came to dominate the Congress. Mr. Bernard Shaw is reported to have said, after meeting Mr. Gandhi, "He is not a man but a phenomenon," and truly it is not easy to explain his astonishing personality; but his achievement in changing the course of Indian history stands clear.

Born of a well-to-do *vaishya* or trading caste Hindu family in western India in October 1869, he was sent to England at the age of nineteen to be trained as a lawyer, and on his return began to practise in Bombay. But in 1893 prospects of a better living took him to South Africa where he remained for over twenty years. There, in defending his fellow countrymen against racial victimization, he evolved the theory and practice of non-violent resistance. Partly it came naturally to him through his Hindu background in which the ancient doctrine of *ahimsa*, the repudiation of force, was accepted, and through the inclinations of his own loving and gentle character; partly it grew through his study of the pacifist writings of Tolstoy, one of his favourite authors, and his appreciation on the one hand of the uselessness of mob violence in the face of modern weapons, and on the other of the effectiveness of mass non-violent resistance against a civilized government. His undoubted spiritual exaltation was usually accompanied in this way by political insight and this unusual combination made him the greatest force in modern Indian politics.

During the First World War, in which Mr. Gandhi had supported Britain's cause, he returned to India and at once made his mark in the National Congress. In his person indeed the main impulses of a generation of Indian religious revivalism and of political agitation came to a head. Brushing aside "mimic Anglicism" he stood forth as an essentially Indian figure and early in 1919 won universal support by taking the lead in denouncing the Government's proposals to pass a series of Bills to suppress the terrorists.

It was a cause after Mr. Gandhi's own heart and he proposed to use his special technique of passive resistance to defeat the Government. Large numbers of Congressmen and of Muslim malcontents, especially in the Punjab, were willing to join forces and, in the excited state of public feeling, sporadic risings took place and simultaneously Afghan tribesmen crossed the frontier into India. For a time it seemed that the administration in the north-west might break down. Martial law was declared and the disorders culminated in a tragic scene at Amritsar where the British military commander directed his troops to break up a large crowd with gunfire; and, although prompt action of this kind had the desired effect of restoring order, a violent outburst of feeling against the Government swept India.

A more unfavourable beginning for the Montagu-Chelmsford constitutional reforms, which became law in December 1919, could hardly have been devised, and it was understandable that the majority of Congressmen should gather round Mr. Gandhi in not only refusing to co-operate in implementing them, but also in threatening to destroy them by non-violent opposition. The "moderates," who thought the reforms should be given a fair trial, quitted the Congress and as "Liberals" took the lead in the provincial and central legislatures. As ministers in charge of the "transferred" departments they made a determined effort in the most difficult circumstances to build parliamentary government in the provinces, but, from the start dubbed "Government men" by their opponents, they generally lacked the essential backing of a strong party in the legislature.

The members themselves showed little tendency to coalesce into coherent, well-organized parties and thus one of the most important conventions of British parliamentary government, the two-party system, did not materialize. Indeed, the National Congress alone at this time possessed the strength to create such organizations. Where parties did emerge—for example, in Madras where the lower caste Hindus united to contest the traditional supremacy of the Brahmans, and in the Punjab, where the Muslims under Fazl-i-Husain formed the Unionist party—they took a religious form; yet, despite the obvious disadvantages of such a basis for the conduct of politics, the system of double government, or dyarchy as it was called, actually proved workable in these circumstances.

In the "transferred" departments in the provinces a number of useful legislative measures, such as the Madras State Aid to Industries Act, 1923, were carried. For the most part the members, knowing that in the last resort they would not be obliged to carry into effect their own policies, took a much more extravagant and outspoken, often irresponsible, point of view than they would otherwise have done, provoking ill-feeling within the Governments and still more extreme sentiments outside them.

Most unfortunate of all for the new ministers was the continued deterioration in the economic situation. Political reforms of this kind obviously demanded some degree of popular support for their successful working; yet in time of financial distress all Governments tend to become unpopular. Retrenchment in the Indian provinces was the order of the day, and the ministers, amid their other difficulties, were compelled to plan "on the cheap," and, however effective the planning, the results rarely looked impressive. On one side alone was a clear gain acknowledged: under the new reforms India achieved fiscal independence and not only framed her own tariff policy, but, in the years following 1919, despite loud protests from British manufacturers, the central government and legislature in complete unanimity imposed a series of duties on British goods, up to twenty per cent, for instance, on Lancashire cottons. Thus, largely at Britain's expense, she began to redress the long-disturbed balance of her economic life.

Other financial proposals met with almost unanimous Indian opposition, particularly the decision in 1923 to balance the budget by doubling the unpopular tax on salt, which already pressed hardest on the poor. On this controversy the Congress decided for the first time to contest the elections, not in order to work the system but avowedly to destroy it by obstruction from within, and from 1924 onwards they used their increasing representation at times, as in Bengal and the Central Provinces, to make it quite impossible for the ministers to hold office, but more often to sustain debates and carry motions demanding from the British Government further and immediate changes in the Indian constitution.

This was particularly true of the Central Legislature, where a tradition of orderly parliamentary procedure was soon created and where common interests often cut across religious antagonisms and carried Mr. Jinnah and his radical Muslim friends into the same lobby as the Hindu Congressmen. Nevertheless, profoundly dissatisfied by the way the reforms were working out and yet determined to abide by their decision to give them a trial run of at least ten years, the Government resisted all change, and unfortunately, although no useful purpose was thereby served, even delayed until 1929 before publicly announcing that Dominion status was "the natural issue of India's constitutional progress."

It would be unfair to criticize harshly the extremely cautious policy of the British Cabinet and Parliament over these years. Indeed, their task had become almost impossible. The British people had not yet recovered from the war, and domestic politics, exacerbated by the general strike of 1926, were troubled. The trends of international affairs, and particularly the collapse of democratic Germany, were doubly confused and confusing and the swift descent of the leading countries into the world economic depression reduced most constructive policies to nought. It was comparatively easy to agree on the most desired ends—lasting peace, full and free national and international trade—but it seemed beyond the wit of statesmen to devise and accept means to these ends. The uncertainty and loss of directness in British policy at home was reflected in her policy abroad, and to Indians it appeared at times that Britain had lost her way and forgotten her purpose.

4. THE MASS REVOLUTIONARY MOVEMENT

India's politicians, in their own affairs seemingly as little able to agree on the means to achieve their aims as the politicians of the west, tended to fix their eyes on the objective, announced in 1919, of complete Indian self-government and, ignoring the necessary, intermediate steps, maintained that there was no good reason why it should not be achieved at once. Gandhi, the Mahatma or "Great Soul" as he universally came to be called, stood out as one of the few who had made a clear decision on political methods. He urged complete pacifism, and his earnestness of purpose, backed by the simplicity and austerity of his personal life, carried conviction among Congressmen. He persuaded them to re-word the first clause of their constitution, to drop the phrase "by constitutional means," and to accept, "The object of the Indian Congress is the attainment of *Swaraj* (self-rule) by the people of India by all legitimate and peaceful means." Although, in his first trials of strength with the British administration, he failed completely to prevent violent outbreaks, and himself admitted that "I knew I was playing with fire," and that he had been guilty of a "Himalayan miscalculation," yet he persisted in extending the range of his "passive resistance" (*satyagraha*). Indeed, his appeal was not to the intellectuals, who had hitherto sustained the struggle for self-rule, but to the mass of Indians, and, his attraction for them, particularly the Hindus, consisting as it largely did in their universal, traditional veneration for the saint, proved magnetic. Trial and imprisonment by the British merely gave him the crown of martyrdom and during the 1920's Mahatma Gandhi in effect succeeded, where Tilak had failed, in changing the middle class nationalist agitation into a mass revolutionary movement.

At the same time he clarified his own philosophy and, with a genius for popular presentation, expressed his ideas in symbolic form. His thinking, always dominated by that part of the mind called the heart, made little pretence at being realistic and he regarded politics not as "the art of the possible" but as the means to social revolution. Feeling that the western world had little of value to give India, particularly that industrialization was an evil, he sought to develop India as a land of villages. The *charkha* or home-made spinning wheel, on which he daily spun cotton thread, became his symbol of a free, simple, rural India needing no military defence and abhorring violence. Through the *charkha* he advocated the wearing of *khaddar*, cloth made from homespun yarn, and the use of *swadeshi*, India-produced articles, in this way not only driving his message to the heart of the countryside but giving Indians a powerful economic method of expressing their political dissatisfaction with the British: and the *charkha* appropriately found a prominent place on the Congress green, white and orange tricolour flag.

Although, on Mahatma Gandhi's word, thousands went to prison or refused to pay their taxes or stood immobile before a charge of police, and tens of thousands changed their way of life, yet, as he well knew, it was impossible to control the more extreme groups or long to keep together the most dissimilar allies. From the start he placed Hindu-Muslim unity at the forefront of his programme and actually joined in supporting the Muslim Khilafat (Caliphate) movement, but although the Muslim leaders and rank and file at first respected him they could not help feeling that the kind of life he led in his *ashram*, or hermitage, and his position as a *guru*, particularly his non-violent policy, marked him as essentially a Hindu rather than a national leader. Moreover, the course of events gave the Muslims seriously to think.

The British Government had duly fulfilled its pledge of 1917 to facilitate the entry of Indians to the higher public services and in the Indian Civil Service, for example, the proportion of British to Indians steadily changed until by 1946 the majority consisted of Indians. Most of the other All-India Services were handed over at the same time to the provincial governments which meant, generally speaking, that British officials were no longer recruited for them. To the rising Hindu and Muslim middle-class groups, the public services, one of the few major "industries" created for them by the British government, had long formed the goal of their ambitions; and to Muslims it seemed that they were placed at a distinct disadvantage by the Hindus' numerical superiority and longer tradition of western learning.

The British decision to divest itself of power in India therefore immediately juxtaposed the Hindus and Muslims not only in an underlying political rivalry, of which the existence of separate electorates was a constant reminder, but also, and equally important, in immediate economic competition. Generally over the whole economic field the Muslims were outclassed: their strength lay among the peasants and the landowning groups, and not in the banking and industrial interests, which were steadily falling under the control of those Hindu groups whose hereditary occupation for centuries had been trade and commerce; the *vaishyas* and *banias* and, among the more prominent, the Marwaris of Rajputana and the Chettys of Madras. Throughout India the contrast between Hindu wealth and Muslim poverty was becoming plain and nowhere more obviously than in Calcutta.

Ill-feeling between the communities rose throughout India and here and there found expression in communal riots, the worst in Calcutta in 1926 when 67 people were killed and over 400 injured. Significantly, the Muslim League, which for some years had dropped into the background, was revived, and in 1928 a group of Hindu politicians, dissatisfied by the Congress profession of neutrality between the two religious communities, organized themselves as the Hindu Mahasabha (Great Assembly) to press caste Hindu interests, and by extension to oppose the Muslims.

This evidence of increasing discord and the known intention of the British Government to review the working of the whole Indian constitution before the ten years' trial (1919–29) had ended, induced a group of the more enlightened leaders of the different parties to confer together early in 1928 and to appoint a committee with Pandit Motilal Nehru, a Kashmiri Brahman and leading Congressman, as chairman and his son, Jawaharlal Nehru, as secretary, to report on the future constitution with special reference to the communal problem. The Committee quickly expressed clear and positive views, first, that Dominion status for India should be "the next, immediate step"; secondly, that the new, responsible Government of India should take over British rights and obligations towards the Indian States, which, it was added, would be welcomed in an Indian Union only if their aristocratic forms of government were modified; and thirdly, that the first stage in settling the communal problem should be the abolition of special electorates.

To these proposals, prompt and equally positive replies came from the groups affected. The majority of Congress at once repudiated Dominion status and declared that a free India outside the Commonwealth was their goal. The Indian princes reserved their right to enter an Indian union and at their own discretion to modify their forms of government. The Muslim League insisted on the retention of separate Muslim electorates and even on the extension of communal representation into the central executive.

And down to the recent acceptance of the partition of India, although the Indian political position has changed continually, these parties did not depart essentially from these decisions.

5. THE SIMON COMMISSION REPORT

The British commission of seven under the chairmanship of Sir John (now Lord) Simon, which was to carry out the promised review of the working of the Montagu-Chelmsford reforms, arrived in India early in 1928, but they received a cool welcome. All parties resented the fact that no Indians had been included in it; and the Congress proclaimed a complete boycott. In spite of all difficulties the investigation was carried out and the Simon Report, produced in 1930, in fact constituted by far the most realistic analysis down to that time of the Indian political problem. The British Government's public promise of Dominion status for India and of its intention to call a Round Table Conference of all Indian groups, including the Indian princes, in London, distracted attention from its findings, but, broadly speaking, they formed the basis of subsequent discussions.

The Commission began by pointing out that the Government's statement on Dominion status had defined British intentions, also that there could be no turning back and that therefore the Commission's sole concern was with the constitutional methods to be adopted. Pointedly it claimed that political developments since 1919 in India—the non-co-operative policy of Congress, the growth of communal feeling and communal parties, the partial failure of the system of provincial dual government—had not justified the faith inspiring the reforms of 1919, but that, nevertheless, because the steps taken could not be retraced, it was more and not less responsible government that was needed. They, therefore, proposed that in the provinces all departments of government should be "transferred" to Indian ministers so that in each province there would be a single ministry responsible, after the British model, to the legislature; the Governor, however, retaining powers—afterwards called "safeguards"—to ensure the safety of the province and the protection of minorities.

The Commission also concluded that communal representation in the legislatures through the system of separate electorates was too firmly rooted to be abolished by the British, even though it marked a complete departure from British parliamentary practice; and it indicated the logical conclusion, namely, that every ministry formed should be a coalition in which at least the major communities would always be represented.

Whereas the Report of 1919 had reached no firm conclusion bout the future form of an All-India Government, the Simon

Commission deemed Federation to be the only practicable mode, even though it felt it would take some time to achieve.

Although the Report thus maintained a positive British policy and gave clear-cut guidance for its fulfilment, underlying all its arguments, and here and there appearing on the surface, there rested a profound doubt on the feasibility of the parliamentary system in India, an opinion which among Indians ensured for the Report an even cooler reception than the Commission itself had received. All Indian parties, indeed, including Congress, were at least agreed on the need for retaining and developing the British parliamentary system.

In the autumn of 1930 to the first Round Table Conference in London were summoned representatives of all Indian parties and of the Indian princes; but so long as Dominion status remained the British target for India, Congress refused to attend, and instead, under Mahatma Gandhi's generalship, launched a widely spreading "civil disobedience" movement, which culminated in violence in all parts of the country. This time, however, unlike 1921, the Muslim community kept aloof, yet, even so, the administration was gravely embarrassed and at times brought to a standstill.

Meanwhile, in London, the representatives of the Indian States at once revealed the willingness of the princes to enter into a federation "with a British India which is self-governing," and the quick endorsement of this by Mr. Jinnah and the Muslim delegates brought an Indian union into the realm of practical politics. The British Government had called the conference in the expectation of approving the findings of the Simon Commission Report, and this early agreement was therefore encouraging, but divisions of opinion on the extension of separate electorates to communities other than the Muslims soon created difficulties, and the obvious absurdity of continuing without the Congress finally led to a special approach being made to Mr. Gandhi through the Viceroy, Lord Irwin. A "pact" was concluded between them, the civil disobedience campaign temporarily called off, and Mr. Gandhi attended the second sitting of the Conference as the sole spokesman of Congress. But his presence complicated rather than clarified the proceedings. No further progress was made towards a decision on the representation of the communities in the legislature, the British Government being finally forced to declare a "communal award." And Mr. Gandhi's express declaration that, as the spokesman of Congress, the only truly national Indian body, he could fairly claim to represent all groups and parties in India including even the Indian States, introduced a new controversy. On his return to India at the close of 1931 the civil disobedience campaign was resumed, and soon afterwards several Congress leaders, including Mr. Gandhi himself, were detained, and the Round Table Conference therefore completed its work without Congress's co-operation.

The conclusions which had been reached through this sifting of the Simon Commission proposals were incorporated in draft proposals, and submitted as the last stage of this prolonged enquiry to a Joint Select Committee of Parliament, whence emerged the Government of India Bill, which was finally passed in 1935.

Appropriately enough it formed the longest Bill in British history and, detailed and difficult a subject though it was, it had certainly taken an excessive time in gestation. This was the more unfortunate because in fact time was the essence of the dispute between the British Government and the Congress. The latter wanted independence: the British were prepared to grant Dominion status, and it was already widely held, and soon to be fully acknowledged, that a Dominion was free to secede from the British Crown and Commonwealth. The difference here was small and therefore the question, "When?" relatively more important. The general British assumption seemed to be that time was on their side, but plainly it was on no man's side for Britain gained nothing by caution and delay, and Indian disunity and exasperation grew with every day that passed. In extenuation it should be said that huge, complicated problems rarely permit of simple, quick solutions. The political future and welfare of three hundred million Indians was at stake. All Britain's political talent was fully engaged on the Bill for many months on end; plainly British statesmen felt the weight of their responsibility, and their seriousness and sincerity of purpose were impressive. In many ways the final achievement was admirable but unhappily it came too late.

6. THE ACT OF 1935

The Act, broadly speaking, dealt with two main subjects, the establishment of an Indian Federation, and secondly, the grant of self-government to the provinces of British India. The first, however, was not to come into being until a specific number of the Indian States had agreed to join; the outbreak of the Second World War in 1939 interrupted the negotiations so that this part of the Act of 1935 was never applied, and the Central Government therefore remained as constituted by the Act of 1919: that is to say, it rested in the hands of the Governor-General in Council, assisted but not controlled by the Council of State and the Central Assembly, and responsible to the British Parliament through the Secretary of State for India.

(a) *The Indian States and Federation*

Although the Indian princes had not hastened to join in creating the Federation it was not so much because they had changed their minds on its general desirability as that, during the course of the Round Table Conferences, they had experienced second and more doubtful thoughts about the likelihood of the Congress forming friendly partners. The hundred or more princes of superior rank and standing had long chafed at their subordinate status in India, and through their meetings in the Chambers of Princes, first inaugurated in 1921, had become much more conscious of their unity of interests and their strength. They knew that their States, scattered like raisins in a cake, covered some two-fifths of the whole of India and included some ninety millions or nearly one-quarter of its total population. The leading States knew that they were larger and more populous than many a sovereign power: Hyderabad, for instance, with some seventeen millions in an area nearly as large as the United Kingdom, and Mysore with seven millions equal in size to Eire. Politically and economically the princes fully appreciated the strategic importance of their position and, aware that British India could not easily get on without them, were not disposed lightly to yield their long cherished hopes of independent rule. Their apprehensions of Congress policy, moreover, were confirmed in 1937. In that year the Congress, which had hitherto concentrated its attention on British India, decided to extend its propaganda throughout the Indian States, and its whole weight was thrown into campaigns for more responsible forms of government in Kashmir in the north, and in Hyderabad, Mysore and Travancore in the south. Particularly in Hyderabad, where the Nizam and the ruling class are Muslim and the mass of the people Hindu, and in Kashmir, where the reverse holds true, communal feelings, excited by the prospect of a complete political and social revolution, quickly rose and led to disturbances. Mr. Gandhi then and later warned the princes that the Congress would soon replace the British as the paramount power in India and that it behoved them at once to come to terms with him, because, as he said, "When I am gone Pandit Jawaharlal Nehru will have no patience with you."

The princes of the larger States, to whom the lesser chiefs looked for a lead, showed a disposition to temporise and in Kashmir, in Hyderabad and in Mysore, representative institutions were enlarged and the general inclination seemed to be to set foot on the road leading to responsible government along which British India had already travelled so far. At the same time many of the princes showed a commendable determination to set and keep their own houses in order: Travancore thus retained her long-held lead in achieving a high standard of adult literacy, the libraries of Baroda became the envy of India, and in irrigation, in the public services, in education and industrialization, Mysore bore comparison with any part of British India.

This excellent work is inspired by the princes' peculiar political outlook. Their ruler-subject relationship, they maintain, is as old as India itself and essentially forms a truer expression of the national genius than the western political institutions of British India. Rightly or wrongly, they believe that their peoples are not yet ready for the full exercise of power.

Doubtless, if one desires complete uniformity of political

institutions in India, it would have been more thoughtful and convenient of the East India Company to have annexed all the Indian States instead of making treaties with and preserving so many. Even if one is tolerant of the continued existence of the States it is obvious that autocracies and democracies cannot easily co-exist in present-day India and that no federation is likely to emerge unless its constituents use similar standards to measure social, economic and political progress. If the princes seek to protect and perpetuate their status, they must adapt themselves, like the British monarchy, to the growth _f democracy; and if this is done India itself is certainly large enough to comprehend and benefit from this degree of variation in her political life.

(b) Provincial self-government 1937–39

The second part of the Act of 1935, unlike the Federation, was carried into effect and has exercised a profound influence on the recent history of India. As proposed by the Simon Commission it provided for Indian self-government in each of the eleven provinces of British India, all the provincial departments of state being transferred to Indian ministers, who were to be responsible to the legislatures. The Governor of each province was to retain powers to safeguard peace and protect the minorities. Lastly, to widen the electoral basis, especially to balance the representation of the town and country, the franchise was extended from the seven millions of 1919 to about thirty-five millions, including six million women and about ten per cent of the "depressed classes," or untouchables. Separate electorates were retained for the Muslims and created also for the Sikhs, Indian Christians, Anglo-Indians and Europeans.

The Act was coolly received in British India partly because all groups had grown sour with waiting. The Muslim leaders expressed a qualified approval of the plan for provincial autonomous constitutions and agreed to participate in working them "for what they were worth," and the Liberals, who had at least saved something from the wreck of the 1919 reforms, volunteered, though without enthusiasm, to play their part again. The Congress which for years had demanded complete independence for India, and saw no reason to change, condemned the Act as a whole and the Governors' retention of special responsibilities, or "safeguards" as they were termed, in particular.

7. THE CONGRESS IN POWER

The lead in the Congress at this time was increasingly being taken by Pandit Jawaharlal Nehru, son of the famous Congressman and Kashmiri Brahman, Motilal, and nominee of Mr. Gandhi as his right-hand man and likely successor. Born in 1889, Mr. Nehru was educated at Harrow and Trinity College, Cambridge, and became a barrister of the Inner Temple, and on his return to India threw himself into the political struggle, in 1921 undergoing the first of many terms of imprisonment which have deeply affected his strongly emotional nature. By far the most attractive to western minds of all living Indians, his forthright speeches and voluminous writings, especially his *Autobiography*, reveal him as one of the greatest English stylists among Indians and also as a socialist, an internationalist and a militant opponent of dictatorship. Deeper still lies his loyalty to Mahatma Gandhi whom he reveres as the maker of Congress, and the architect of Indian independence. Time and again, and not always with the happiest results, he has modified his own strong views to conform with Mr. Gandhi's lead; and with the latter's approval he became President of the Congress in 1936 and 1937. It was Mr. Nehru's privilege to bring into full action the machine which Mahatma Gandhi had created.

Pandit Nehru urged that both in the elections for the central legislatures (which, failing the creation of the Federation, were still constituted as in 1919) and for the provincial governments the National Congress should take part "not to co-operate in any way with the Act but to combat it and seek the end of it"; and in fact in the voting for the Central Assembly in 1935 the Congress achieved the strongest single party. Indeed, there was no other political organization in India to compare with it in strength or discipline. The All-

I

India Muslim League, which mainly represented the not very politically active Muslim land-owning classes, was still a negligible force and in the process of being reorganized by a leading Muslim lawyer, Mr. Muhammad Ali Jinnah, of Bombay, who had long taken a prominent part in its affairs and had in 1934 become its permanent president.

Born in 1876 Mr. Jinnah, like Mr. Nehru, was trained in England, and on his return to India joined the Congress, but finding Mr. Gandhi's policies and methods, especially his civil disobedience movements, quite unacceptable he soon moved over to the Muslim League. Nevertheless, Mr. Jinnah remained convinced that co-operation with the Congress was desirable and possible in the common task of ridding India of the British, and his sincerity had so impressed his contemporaries that in Pandit Nehru's *Autobiography*, published in 1937, reference was made to him as "the ambassador of Hindu-Muslim unity." On this conviction he led the Muslim delegates in the Central Assembly—even though by so doing he incurred the suspicion of the more conservative Muslims—and with the same intentions he took the Muslim League into the provincial elections which were held in 1937.

Of the eleven provinces of British India in which the first elections under the terms of the 1935 Act took place, the North West Frontier and Sind were overwhelmingly Muslim in population. In the adjacent Punjab fifty-seven per cent of the people were Muslims, the rest being Hindus and Sikhs. In Bengal, Muslims constituted fifty-five per cent of the population, the rest consisting mainly of Hindus. In each of the other seven provinces the Hindus had a very large majority; and thus taking British India as a whole the Hindus, including the scheduled castes, formed sixty-five per cent as against the Muslims twenty-seven per cent of the total population. That being so and with the Congress operating the only effective country-wide, electioneering machine, it was a foregone conclusion that in the Hindu majority provinces, the Congress would lead the poll; but, in fact, the results of the elections went further and formed a striking demonstration of the strength and appeal of the Congress under Mahatma Gandhi and Pandit Nehru, not only in the towns but in the countryside too.

Congress members achieved clear majorities in six provinces. Also, in the overwhelmingly Muslim North West Frontier Province, the Red Shirt movement, which identified itself with Congress policy, carried the day.

The Congress did not expect to, and did not in fact, prevail in the Muslim-majority provinces of Bengal, the Punjab and Sind. In these three, where the Muslims were divided amongst themselves, and in Assam, too, where politics were confused by the existence of many small parties, coalition governments, in which Muslims predominated, were formed but in the other provinces the question was whether the Congress would take office after all.

After some months' hesitation, and after challenging and being reassured on the British interpretation of the Governors' "safeguards," the Congress, despite their previous declarations and Mr. Nehru's misgivings, finally agreed in the summer of 1937 to form Congress ministries in their seven majority provinces. In taking this decision they firmly rejected the alternative, for which Mr. Jinnah had long striven and on which he had based his election campaign, of forming Congress-Muslim League coalition ministries.

This fateful choice, which marks a turning point in the recent history of India, arose directly from the character and policy of the Congress. The Congress was, and is, a national organization including members of all Indian religious communities, and drawing its funds from all economic groups from the poorest of untouchables to the biggest of "big business men." Under Mahatma Gandhi and Pandit Nehru it had reached out and inspired ignorant peasants and young intellectuals alike and it claimed to speak for and represent all Indians. All who could afford four annas (4½d.) a year, and who believed in "the attainment by the people of India of complete independence by all legitimate and peaceful means" could join it; and it was said in 1938 that over four million had done so, thus giving Congress the claim to be the largest political organization in the world. But more important than figures is the fact that most Indians look to the Congress for a lead and regularly support its policies.

The members of the Congress yearly nominate their

delegates—some 2,000—whose duty it is to elect the President and to attend the famous annual session, which lasts about a week, and which, in its essential simplicity and general atmosphere of a large and gay fun fair, provides one of the most astonishing political sights of the world. The President on election enjoys the right to nominate fourteen members to form his Working Committee, more popularly termed "The High Command," which under him then assumes control of Congress affairs. From the time when in 1934, at the age of sixty-five, Mahatma Gandhi began to retire for increasingly long periods to his *ashram*, or hermitage, at Sevagram, Pandit Nehru has dominated the Working Committee, but always subject, especially at times of crisis, to the intervention and approval of Gandhi himself, whose hold on the popular imagination persisted.

With a long tradition of successful agitation, with a country-wide and national organization, which had just demonstrated its strength and discipline in the elections, and with a closely unified central control of policy, the Working Committee in 1937 saw no reason why, within a few years, the Congress should not wholly replace the British *Raj*. In its view there was no justification whatsoever for acceding to Mr. Jinnah's proposal to form coalition governments with the Muslim League, the more so because the latter was merely one, and not necessarily the most important, of a number of Muslim parties. To the Working Committee much the more practical policy, especially in view of the support which the Congress was enjoying from the so-called "Redshirt" Muslims under Abdul Ghaffar Khan in the North West Frontier Province, seemed to be to attempt to absorb the Muslim League along with most other small Indian parties. The past history of Hindu-Muslim relations might indeed indicate that a compromise with the Muslim League would form a more prudent and generous policy, but the tide of success was running so strongly in 1937 in Congress's favour that the Working Committee felt that the bolder plan offered not so much a gamble as a certainty. In fact, it completely miscalculated.

Mortified by a personal sense of slight and humiliated by this public rebuff to a policy he had pursued for years, Mr.

Jinnah rejected the Congress claim that, if he and his League wanted a share in government, they must be absorbed into Congress and in effect submit to the control of its Hindu majority. Acceptance of that view, he felt, would amount to political suicide and rather he set himself to rally the whole Muslim community behind the Muslim League; and the developing policy of the Congress played into his hands.

The Congress one-party ministries duly took office in the seven provinces and, broadly speaking, in the strict way in which they maintained law and order, in the zeal with which they pressed on a much-needed policy of agrarian reform, and in the efficiency and skill with which they managed financial matters, they fully justified their existence. Understandably the eyes of the Congress ministers in the provinces turned for guidance to the Working Committee, with its mass country-wide support and a fifty years' tradition behind it, rather than to the newly created and as yet untried legislatures. Understandably, too, on its side, the Working Committee, pursuing a "national" policy and aware of the diverse and even conflicting interests of different regions in so large a country as India, sought to exercise a rigid discipline over all the Congress ministries; and, significantly, Mr. Jawaharlal Nehru, Dr. Rajendra Prasad and other members of the Committee chose to remain outside the provincial ministries and to direct affairs from the Congress centre at Wardha.

In consequence of these converging tendencies the Congress ministries as a group assumed an extraordinary coherence of policy and tended to act as though they were responsible not to their own electorates but to the Congress "high command." Thus the first true attempt to apply British parliamentary democracy to India at once produced a system which was not recognizably British. This was inevitable for it would be absurd to expect English political institutions in India to develop exactly after the English pattern. Indeed, John Stuart Mill, who in the previous century had given considerable thought to the extension overseas of English representative government, had aptly appreciated this possibility and had maintained that good government in India would have to be based on "far wider political conceptions than merely English or European practice can supply." In the vast area covered by the widely-scattered provinces of British India, some consistency and coherence of policy in any one party spread through these provinces is desirable, and, looking to the future, also necessary if a high rate of social and economic progress is to be maintained on a country-wide basis. Between 1937 and 1939 the Congress leaders could not exercise control through the Central Government, which in essentials still rested in British hands, and they therefore chose to operate instead from their own party headquarters.

More disturbing for the future of India was the danger that the Congress organization might altogether supplant the state machinery; but here again nothing is so little useful as arguing by analogy from England. The Congress is not a party in the Western sense but a political mass movement; a congeries of parties including for instance a strong socialist wing and an influential capitalist group, which will almost certainly begin to assert their separate independence and policies when any consolidation of Congress power takes place. In England political parties evolved within and conformed to the needs of Parliament; in India the Congress, which grew first, looms larger than the legislatures and therefore for some time to come is bound to encompass and condition the growth of parliamentary institutions.

8. THE MUSLIM REACTION

Although the Congress sincerely strove to develop a national policy it could not disguise the fact that it drew its main strength from the caste Hindus and that essentially Hindu modes of thought and conduct had exercised a determining influence on its history. As we have seen, Muslim leaders had never for long become reconciled to any one of the various stages in the growth of the Congress, and in 1937 they were thoroughly alarmed by the completeness of its electoral victory, and by its rejection of the idea of coalition governments. These developments, accompanied by the Congress claim to represent all Indians including Muslims, and ultimately to replace the British, recalled to Muslim minds the dire prophecies of Sir Sayyid Ahmad about their likely fate under a Hindu *Raj*, and pouring in from every side soon came confirmation of their worst suspicions. Three Muslim Reports appeared in quick succession between 1937 and 1939 accusing Hindu Congressmen in office not only of general discrimination against Muslims but also of particular atrocities and, although it was impossible to prove most of them, *the fact was* that the Muslims believed them to be true. And as justification for their belief they could point to the growing strength of the Hindu Mahasabha, a notoriously anti-Muslim association.

Muslim landowners, too, became apprehensive of the Congress agrarian policy, which was promising so much to the peasants that it could only be given at the expense of the landlords. But, most important of all, the Muslim middle classes as a whole foresaw a bleak future with themselves relegated to an inferior position whether in the public services, in the professions or in industry. They had long recognized and strongly resented their community's educational back-wardness compared with the Hindus, and therefore were particularly sensitive to the Congress educational policy, especially its excellent scheme of primary instruction through handicrafts, a product of Mr. Gandhi's mind and largely coloured by Hindu associations. The cry soon arose that even Muslim culture was being attacked by the Congress; and that to attack their culture was to threaten their life. This modern communal struggle, in essence arising through a middle class Hindu and Muslim rivalry for political and economic power, naturally took the simplest expression of a more general religious conflict, and riots began to break out with such frequency that it seemed a sporadic civil war had started.

Mr. Jinnah stood forth as the champion of these Muslim views. It was a crime, he declared, that a quarter of India's population should be treated in this fashion but, "the Muslims," he added, "can expect neither justice nor fair play under Congress government." Between 1937 and 1939 he experienced a swift rise to power on this wave of Muslim fear until he was accepted as not merely one among a number but *the* leader of the Muslim community and his organization, the League, as *the* representative Muslim body.

The Congress policy in fact had turned the Muslim League for the first time in its history into an effective political force. The Muslim prime ministers of the Punjab, Bengal and Assam declared that they would henceforth back the League and advised all their supporters at once to become members; and soon the control exercised by Mr. Jinnah from the League headquarters over the Muslim-led ministries of the Punjab and Bengal compared with that exerted by the Congress over its ministries. In their operation of parliamentary institutions there was evidently little to choose between the rival organizations. From 1937 onwards, in by-elections to the Central and Provincial Legislatures, the Muslim League gained the great majority of Muslim seats; and in the general election of 1946 it became plain that the Muslim League carried the support of over ninety per cent of the Muslims of British India.

Mr. Jinnah's own policy simultaneously underwent a revolution; and from acceptance of the Act of 1935 he swung back to Sir Sayyid Ahmad's theme: English parliamentary government, he now declared, with its emphasis on majority rule and the maintenance of a strong central government, would permanently subordinate the Muslims to a Hindu Congress and was therefore unsuited to India. Echoing the words of Sir Sayyid, he proclaimed in 1940, "There are in India two nations," and that in fact only a separate, national homeland would remove Muslim fears and satisfy their demands. A decade earlier, when presiding over the Muslim League, Sir Muhammad Iqbal, the famous poet of Pan-Islamism, had urged the consolidation of the Muslim provinces of the north-west, not as a sovereign, independent state but as part of a loose federation of all India; and this idea had been endorsed in greater detail in 1939 by Sir Sikandar Hyat Khan, the Premier and foremost Muslim statesman of the Punjab. A proposal for out and out Partition, however, had been advocated in 1933 by a group of young Muslim students in England who formed what they called "The Pakistan National Movement," and although little notice was taken of them at the time—indeed a Muslim League spokesman dismissed their scheme as "chimerical and impracticable"—

U . S . S . R

AFGHANISTAN

PERSIA (IRAN)

BALUCHISTAN

N.W. FRONTIER

KASHMIR

PUNJAB

SIND

DELHI

RAJPUTANA STATES

UNITED PROVINCES

NEPAL

TIBET

SIKKIM

ASSAM

BIHAR

BENGAL

BURMA

KATHIAWAR

CENTRAL PROVINCES

BOMBAY

ORISSA

HYDERABAD

GOA

MYSORE

MADRAS

COORG

TRAVANCORE

CEYLON

INDIA
WITH THE AREAS CLAIMED
FOR PAKISTAN
ROUGHLY INDICATED BY SHADING

ENGLISH MILES

0   100 200 300 400 500

"GEOGRAPHIA" Lᵀᴰ

it was essentially their idea that was finally taken up by Mr.
Jinnah and put forward in March, 1940, as representing the
Muslim League's point of view. A separate, independent state
called Pakistan (meaning "Land of the Pure") was demanded,
consisting of the Muslim majority regions of the Punjab, of
the Frontier Province and Sind in the north-west, and of
Bengal (including Assam) in the north-east. With this formal
declaration the Muslim reaction to the Congress was complete,
and partition had become the fundamental issue of Indian
politics!

9. THE WARTIME DEADLOCK

Meanwhile, in September 1939 the Second World War
had begun and Britain, as in 1914, took India to war with her.
But the Congress Working Committee, which had for some
years anticipated such a situation, was determined not to miss
this opportunity of achieving its main goal. Arguing that a
country which was not yet itself free could hardly be called on
to defend freedom, they demanded immediate and complete
independence for India as the terms of Congress's co-operation
in the war effort. When the Viceroy countered by reaffirming
Britain's promise of Dominion status, the Working Committee
exercised its hold over the Congress provincial ministries by
calling them out of office. The Muslim League's response to
this was to organize "a day of deliverance and thanksgiving,"
but in its attitude to the war, although allowing its members
individually to co-operate with Britain, it, too, offered its
support only on terms, namely, that the Congress plans for India
should be rejected and that Muslims alone should determine
their own constitutional future.

Several new approaches by the Viceroy met with the same
response and the deadlock thus established by the Congress
and League's contrary demands persisted until after the end of
the war. Most of the Congress leaders, especially Pandit
Nehru, wanted to help China against Japan, and Russia against
Germany but were inhibited by the fact that they would have
to act under the British. Their sense of frustration went deep—
how deep may be seen from Jawaharlal Nehru's *Discovery of*

India written in prison between 1942 and 1945—and in large part it explains their increasingly bitter attacks on Britain.

Whilst the fighting remained remote from India, Britain's war effort in the East was not seriously impeded; the munitions industries steadily expanded and the volunteer armies rose to over two millions, the largest in history. But when Japan entered the war in December 1941, and, slicing easily through the defences of Singapore and Burma, stood on the threshold of India, it became imperative at once to attempt to rally the moral support of the major political groups, particularly the Congress, behind the soldiers, sailors and airmen defending the frontiers and coasts. The British war cabinet therefore hastily despatched one of its members, Sir Stafford Cripps, to make a new offer. In return for the immediate support of the major Indian political parties, which were to be represented in a new central government, Britain proposed, as soon as the war was over, to give India complete freedom and self-government in a Union which could accept Dominion status within the Commonwealth or not as it chose; and that the constitution should be made by a body consisting of nominees of the Indian states and elected representatives of the provincial legislatures. To meet the Muslim case, it was proposed that any Indian provinces which wished to contract out of the proposed Union might do so and form a separate Union of equal status.

This most realistic appreciation of the political and military situation went far towards meeting the most important Indian demands, and although the Congress was not happy at the prospect of the possible secession of the predominantly Muslim provinces, and the League was disappointed that an outright grant of Pakistan had not been made, they both knew that the essential facts in the Indian situation had been recognized. The offer indeed might well have been accepted but the Congress asked also for the immediate establishment at the centre of "a National Government [which] must be a Cabinet Government with full power," and this the British Government, with the Japanese at the gate, rightly decided was impracticable. "The Congress," as Sir Stafford Cripps said, "wanted all or nothing." They had long sought complete independence and were not willing to accept it in instalments. Independence first and discussion of details afterwards was their topsy-turvy demand, and they were encouraged in this by the thought that, from the way the fighting was going, Britain would hardly be in a position at the end of the war to redeem her promises. "A post-dated cheque on a bank that is obviously failing," was Mr. Gandhi's reported description of the offer, and in that mood it was rejected, and a call made to Britain to "quit India" under threat of the last and greatest of Mahatma Gandhi's non-violent campaigns. "There is no question," he said, "of one more chance. After all this is open rebellion." In this critical situation the Government of India, which now consisted of fifteen British and eleven Indian members besides the Viceroy, waited for some weeks in the hope that cooler counsels might prevail; but, when Mr. Gandhi's lead was formally accepted by the Congress, they unanimously decided on firm action. The Congress was declared an unlawful association and once again Mr. Gandhi and its leaders were interned. An outbreak of violence and sabotage ensued. It was fiercest in Bihar where the communications of the troops defending the eastern frontier with their main sources of supply were cut, but in a few weeks the worst was over, and by the end of 1942 order was restored.

The "Cripps offer" remained open but the Muslim League too had finally turned it down, and, for the rest of the war, whilst her soldiers gained the admiration of the world, frustration and despair gripped the hearts of India's politicians; and, although in 1945 the Congress leaders were released, renewed attempts at compromise broke down. The protracted manœuvring for position produced a rising crescendo of riots and India's leaders from Mahatma Gandhi downwards began to talk ominously and hopelessly of civil war.

10. INDEPENDENCE AND CIVIL STRIFE

The accession to power of a Labour Government in Britain in the late summer of 1945 and the collapse of Japan produced a clearer atmosphere in which the British cabinet, well aware that further delay might result in a catastrophe, took the unprecedented and boldly imaginative step of sending three of its foremost ministers, including Sir Stafford Cripps, to break the deadlock. The Cripps mission had already demonstrated Britain's sincerity, the cabinet mission left no doubt about its determination to hand over responsibility for the government of India to Indians.

The process of achieving agreement between the Indian parties, first by fruitless mediation and then, in May 1946, by making direct British proposals, was tortuous, but it rested on the steadily held British belief that the division of India between sovereign states could be avoided while giving adequate protection to Muslim interests. A British long-term proposal was made which, by an ingenious and constructive modification of the Cripps offer, contemplated the establishment of an Indian Union, arranged in three tiers of authorities. At the top, the Central Government was to control defence, foreign affairs and communications; and to consist of an executive and a legislature drawn from British India and (after negotiation) the Indian states. At the bottom, the provinces, enjoying a wide measure of self-government, were to constitute another tier, and thirdly, as a possible midway tier, if any of them so chose they could form themselves into provincial groups with their own executives and legislatures; and each group was to determine the subjects, outside those reserved for the Central Government, which it wished to control in common. The Cabinet mission proposed also that the constitution-making process should start with the calling of a Constituent Assembly representing all parties.

This fair and feasible plan offered the means by which, if they so desired, the Congress and Muslim League could preserve a united India and yet achieve the reality of Pakistan. In the meantime, to show that Britain meant business, the Viceroy, Lord Wavell, was authorized at once to negotiate with the major parties to form a *de facto* responsible interim Government in which all cabinet posts would be held by Indians. As the negotiations proceeded, the struggle for power between the Congress and the Muslim League was reflected in large scale riots and massacres, surpassing in magnitude anything previously known in modern Indian history. Within six months in Bihar and Bengal alone over ten thousand men, women and children suffered violent deaths. The turmoil reached a new height when first the Muslim League alone and then Congress alone undertook to form the interim Government, and it still continued when in October 1946 both parties at last came together in the same Indian cabinet. The Indian leaders themselves had for so long been accustomed to acting irresponsibly and their minds were so grooved in the psychology of opposition that they found it difficult to adjust their conduct to their new status: and although they had formed a joint cabinet little desire to co-operate with their opponents was shown by either of the main parties.

On 2 September 1946, in the Council Room of the Viceroy's House at Delhi, Lord Wavell administered the oath of allegiance to the first members of a wholly responsible, Indian cabinet and thus completed a major revolution in the political life of India. And outside, perhaps aware that a desperate struggle was just beginning, the riotous crowds were surging, some shouting, "Victory to Hindustan! Long live Congress!" and others defiantly answering, "Death to Congress! Long live Pakistan!"

.   .   .   .   .

Thus a fifty-years' struggle reached its tragic climax. Responsibilities for the course of events were widely distributed; English education, based on the English language, inevitably led Indians to demand parliamentary government, but Britain had not given a clear direction to constitutional development in India until 1919, when it was almost too late, and thereafter acted slowly; the Congress had rejected the Muslim League's offer of co-operation in 1937 and thereafter set out to dominate all parties and all India; and between 1937 and 1940 the Muslim League had grown up in fear and thereafter, through fear, closed its mind to the wider interests of Indians and set itself to break the hard-won unity of India.

CHAPTER VI

THE PARTITION OF INDIA
1947

THE British Cabinet Mission's proposals of May, 1946, sought to maintain the unity of India. To the British, who had created an outward Indian unity and within it proudly preserved a *pax Britannica*, it seemed clear that Indians, living in a poor, largely agricultural country on the margin of existence, could ill afford to lose the advantages of economic union, and that India, with a well-trained army and a growing industry, should use its united strength to reinforce the regional defences of the Indian Ocean. Appreciating at the same time that internal politics loomed larger to Indians than the broader problems of economics and strategy, the British short-term plan of drawing the Congress and Muslim League leaders into the same interim cabinet was shrewdly conceived; thus, it was hoped that through working together in solving common problems they would grow to tolerate one another.

Before many days had passed it became obvious that the plan was failing. The Muslim League soon revealed that it had decided to participate only to prevent the Congress from controlling the Centre. Both sides continually charged the Viceroy with partiality and the impossible situation emerged in which neither party desired to continue the artificial partnership, yet neither was willing to resign; and each was hanging on hoping to bluff the other out of office. When the Constituent Assembly, which under the Cabinet Mission's long-term plan was to frame the constitution of the projected Union of India, met at Delhi in December 1946, the failure of the experiment in bi-partisan government was made obvious by the Muslim League's point-blank refusal to take part and its demand for an indefinite postponement. Although the Congress members of the Assembly boldly pressed on with its work —not the least part of which included a definition of human rights, a formal abolition of untouchability and a declaration that

India was to be a sovereign, independent republic—the debates sounded hollow and the decisions unreal. All the resolutions taken were duly denounced by the Muslim League as "*ultra vires*, invalid and illegal," and in the circumstances the Indian princes, whose states also should have been represented, could hardly be blamed for hesitating to join the Assembly.

The British cabinet, magnificently determined to retain its hard-won initiative, strove once more to break the deadlock by inviting Pandit Nehru and Mr. Jinnah, each with a party colleague, and also the Sikh leader, Sardar Baldev Singh, to London for further discussions, the main outcome of which on their return to India was an open demand by the Congress for either the immediate entry of the Muslim League into the Constituent Assembly or its resignation from the interim Government.

Throughout this time of stress most of India's leaders showed themselves lacking in a proper sense of responsibility. Truly, in seizing the petty, tactical advantage they frequently revealed insight, but of foresight they gave little evidence. Indeed, through their early training in the West and their later, troubled experiences in India, many of them were like men adrift between two worlds; unstable, irresponsible, outspoken, they could not escape from the conditioning effect of years of opposition to a strong Government, and it was perhaps asking too much of them that they should have shown a quicker understanding of their opponents' point of view and a will to pacific compromise. The Muslim League fearfully persisted in seeking its ends through assertion rather than discussion, and the Congress, although much the stronger party, showed little magnanimity. They all knew the dangers they were running yet they seemed not to have the capacity to visualize the consequences of civil strife. Thus forces were let loose among the highly emotional Indian masses which could not be controlled, and blood-letting, killing, torture, abduction, rape, all the horrors of civil war, occurred on a large scale.

The worst affected area was the Punjab, a province which, although mixed in its communities, had long and proud traditions of efficient, orderly government. Trouble started there when the Unionist Coalition Ministry, which had held office since 1937, made the justifiable but ill-timed decision to ban private armies, whether Muslim or Hindu. The Muslim League at once seized on this as a heaven-sent opportunity for ridding the heartland of Pakistan of what was to them a palpably inconvenient Coalition Government, and proclaimed in February 1947 a campaign of "non-violence" and "courting of arrest" which, being interpreted by the Hindus and Sikhs as an attempt to seize power, quickly degenerated into persistent rioting and fighting. In the next few months according to official statistics alone over five thousand men, women and children in the Punjab were killed or injured; the flourishing towns of Amritsar and Multan went up in flames; the work of the capital, Lahore, came to a standstill, and roving armed bands in the countryside fought pitched battles with the troops.

Once again, to save India despite herself, the British Government intervened, this time bluntly attempting to shock India's leaders into some sort of agreement by declaring that the promised transfer of power from British to Indian hands must be completed by June 1948. In short, responsibility was publicly placed on Indian shoulders, and as if to point the moral that a new start was imperative Lord Wavell was replaced by a new Viceroy, Viscount Mountbatten, recently the Allied Supreme Commander in South-East Asia.

A burst of friendliness towards Britain in the Indian press indicated some recognition of her sincerity and willingness to go to the extreme limit in trying to give India's leaders a clear field in which to mould India's political future. But the new declaration in fact had answered neither the Congress demand for the dismissal of the five Muslim League members from the interim Government nor the League's claim that the Constituent Assembly was illegal; neither did it indicate the steps or the time-table by which the delicate and intricate operation of withdrawing from India was to be effected, nor to which Indian Governments power was to be handed. Indeed the whole proposal was dangerously vague, encouraging obstructionism among the communal vested interests and setting a premium on disunity.

Nevertheless with each day that passed, with each fresh

K

outbreak of communal fighting, it was becoming clear that the British administration could no longer guarantee law and order; and British dominion in India which had begun in the eighteenth century with the wide exercise of power divorced from responsibility, seemed likely to come to an ignominious end through accepting responsibility far in excess of its power to enforce. Therefore in justification of the British declaration it might be urged that a desperate remedy alone was adequate to so desperate a situation.

In the event Mr. Jinnah's prompt answer was uncompromising,—"The Muslim League will not yield an inch in its demand for Pakistan"—and, as if to echo his words, the communal war in the Punjab mounted to its climax, the Unionist Government resigned, and, on the League's failure to form a ministry and refusal to consider the possibility of a Coalition, the Governor reluctantly took over the administration.

The Congress Working Committee members, sickened at last by what Pandit Nehru called "the politics . . . of jungle warfare" and profoundly shocked by what Mahatma Gandhi damned as "India's mad career of violence," began to reach the conclusion that if the unity of India could be preserved only through civil war and the exercise of force—and the British had made it clear that it would have to be Congress and not British force—then the price was too high to pay. Prompted by suggestions from their own local parties in Bengal and the Punjab they therefore responded to the British declaration by proposing in May, 1947, the partition of the Punjab as a solution of the grim struggle there. This decision, revealing in them a hitherto unsuspected flexibility of mind and willingness to compromise, did them great credit because at that juncture it cannot have been easy for fervent nationalists to abandon their traditional and fundamental policy. It not only justified the shock tactics of the British Government but at once brought the partition of all-India into the realm of practical politics.

The new Viceroy, squarely facing the realities of the situation, turned over the whole matter with the main party leaders, quickly drew his conclusions, and promptly flew to London there to hustle the cabinet along with him. Within a

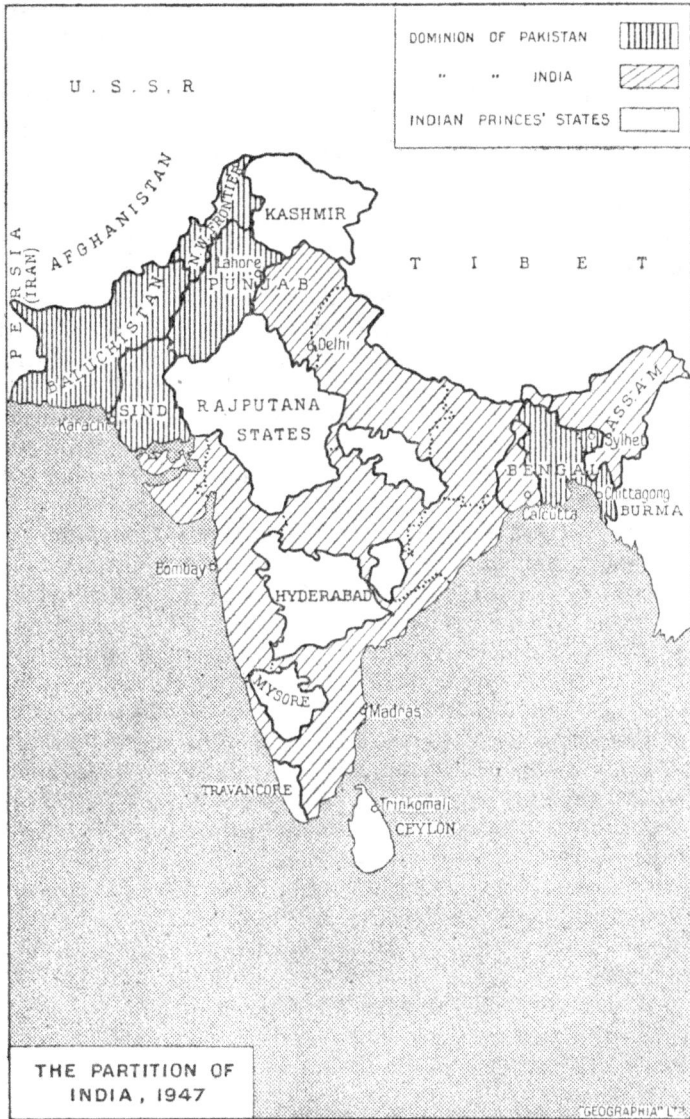

THE PARTITION OF
INDIA, 1947

fortnight they produced "a procedural plan" which in effect provided for the immediate partition of India and which on the day of its announcement (3 June) gained the assent, albeit unwilling, of the Muslim League, the Congress, and the Sikhs. With equal suddenness the communal fighting died down to manageable proportions and overnight the Indian political scene changed for the better.

In the crisis of 1942, when the Japanese armies reached the frontiers of India, the "Cripps offer" suggesting partition had been rejected by all Indian parties; in 1947, when communal disorders threatened to disrupt the state, the somewhat similar "Mountbatten offer" was at once accepted. The tragic events of the intervening years had proved that the Hindu-Muslim struggle for power, especially in the Punjab and Bengal provinces where the communities were mixed and evenly balanced, had grown so fierce that only consummate Indian statesmanship or partition could provide the necessary breathing space in which passions might cool and saner counsels prevail. The British acted properly and raised their political reputation high in these years, first in giving India's leaders their rightful opportunity to work together and then, on their evident failure, in returning to the idea of partition.

Briefly, the plan allowed for the division of the Punjab and Bengal—in each of which there were small Muslim majorities—into Hindu and Muslim states, the effective decision for this being taken by each Legislative Assembly, voting if necessary by separate communities. Boundary commissions in the two provinces were provided to draw the exact frontiers partly "on the basis of ascertaining the contiguous majority areas of Muslims and non-Muslims" and partly taking into account other factors such as communications, resources and the Punjab irrigation system. In Sind, too, the Legislative Assembly was required to say whether it wished to join Pakistan.

In the overwhelmingly Muslim N.W. Frontier Province, in which by a curious paradox a strong pro-Congress party, the 'Red Shirts' under Abdul Ghaffar Khan, had held office since 1937, a referendum was provided to allow the population to state which political group they wanted to belong to; and similarly the Muslim-majority district of Sylhet in south Assam was invited to say whether it wished to join East Bengal in forming the second new Muslim state.

Without a major hitch, the plan was swiftly carried through and thus out of the former provinces of British India two independent Dominions of Pakistan and India, each free and equal and of no less status than the United Kingdom, and each with its own Constituent Assembly, came into existence. Pakistan consisted of a Muslim state in the north-west, including Sind and the Frontier Province which had voted to join, and of a Muslim state in East Bengal, including Sylhet which had followed the Frontier Province's example. The second new Dominion, which retained the name "India," covered the rest of what had been British India. These two sovereign powers duly took their place in the Commonwealth, naturally enjoying with their sister Dominions the right to secede at their own discretion.

The title of Emperor of India held by the British Crown since 1876 lapsed; and India nominated, as its first Governor-General, Viscount Mountbatten, whilst Pakistan chose Mr. Jinnah; and under them the complicated tasks of dividing the powers, rights, assets, property, liabilities and not least the Indian army itself, and of withdrawing the British forces were carried through. Simultaneously, the conduct of British relations with India and Pakistan was undertaken by the Secretary of State for Commonwealth Relations and the historic office of Secretary of State for India came to an end.

The position of the Indian princes was at first left undetermined. As had previously been announced the paramountcy of the British Crown over them lapsed and, because Dominion status was closed to them, they were left free to seek association with or independence of the two new powers. A number of them—Mysore, the Rajputana states as well as Patiala, Baroda, Gwalior, Cochin, and the newly-formed confederation of Kathiawar and Gujerat states—for geographical and communal reasons ranged themselves with the new India. Others, such as Bhopal, where a Muslim Nawab ruled a majority of Hindu subjects in the midst of the new Dominion of India, hesitated before following suit and

Kashmir, contiguous with Pakistan and with a Muslim majority yet ruled by a Hindu prince, found it difficult to make a decision. One of the most powerful rulers, the Nizam of Hyderabad, took the bull by the horns and announced his intention of declaring his independence. In the face of these different choices the representative Chamber of Princes, which had outlived its usefulness, dissolved itself, but all the princes were at one in challenging those Congressmen who took it for granted that the states could not long hope to survive the departure of the British; and, by the steps many of them took increasingly to associate their peoples with them in government, they declared their faith in the states' future. Nevertheless, their contacts with British India have long been so close that there is no reason to doubt that the states, with the possible exceptions of Kashmir and Hyderabad, will freely associate with one or other of the new Dominions.

By 15 August 1947, after the quick passage of the Indian Independence Act which was acclaimed in India as "the noblest act and greatest law ever enacted by the British Parliament," the partition of India was a fact. It represented a state of affairs which had come to pass largely through Muslim fear and Hindu despair. It opened India to the dangers of political, economic and strategic "balkanization." But equally it represented a political masterstroke which at the last minute saved India from widespread civil war. Besides once more demonstrating the political ability of the British, it set the two new Indian powers in the wider community of the Commonwealth, thus reserving for India's leaders another chance to save and later restore some Indian unity.

The British Prime Minister, Mr. Attlee, who deserves so well of India, and who with Sir Stafford Cripps has done so much to restore Britain's reputation for sincerity and political wisdom throughout the East, spoke truly and for the whole Commonwealth when introducing the Indian Independence Act, "I earnestly hope," he said, "that this severance may not endure, that the two new Dominions we now propose to set up may in the course of time come together again to form one great member-state of the British Commonwealth of Nations—but this is a matter for Indians themselves."

CHAPTER VII

INDIA'S DEEPER PROBLEMS

I. THE CONTRADICTIONS OF PARTITION

THE Muslims of India form a nation apart from the Hindus in that they *feel* themselves to be a separate nation, and no plan for the government of India which ignores this fact can last: Muslim fear of Hindu domination is too strong, and Hindu-Muslim antagonism too closely associated with the more fundamental Indian problems of poverty and mass ignorance to be dismissed. Yet it does not follow that such nationhood entitles the Muslims to create and perpetuate a separate state. National aspirations, as the Scots and Welsh in Britain and the French and Germans in Switzerland have proved, can be otherwise satisfied. Both Pakistan and the Indian Union face social and economic problems which are common to both and which demand common solutions; a process which would offer the best opportunity of outgrowing the more superficial rivalries. The peculiar merit of the British Cabinet Mission's proposal of May 1946 was that it fulfilled the immediate need of recognizing and in essence satisfying the Muslims' desire for a valid political and territorial embodiment of their sense of separate nationhood without at the same time disrupting the economic and strategic unity of India.

Under the Partition Plan of 1947 a second, if somewhat less favourable, opportunity of working together opens itself to the two new Dominions within the framework of the Commonwealth, and the responsibility for the future of India rests squarely on the shoulders of Indian leaders.

The emergence of Pakistan as a sovereign state certainly clears away some short-term political difficulties; it diminishes the threat of countrywide civil war; it reduces the Muslims' fear of permanent Hindu domination and ministers to their pride by broadening their political footing not only in India but also, as a member of the group of Middle Eastern Muslim states, in the world at large. Furthermore, the Muslim League feels that the existence of a Muslim majority state in India not merely satisfies the self-respect of the Pakistani Muslims, but also provides a safeguard, on the crude argument of "an eye for an eye" and "a life for a life," for the Muslims left in the Hindu majority state. In fact the newly-drawn boundaries have left some forty millions of Muslims in the Union of India, as compared with about twenty millions of Hindus as a minority in Pakistan. Moreover, the sturdy warrior Sikhs, four millions strong in the heart of the Punjab, detest the thought of, and will resist the fact of, their own inclusion, wholesale or in part, within Pakistan. Indeed, every argument for Pakistan as a solution of a minority problem is also an argument against it; and all responsible persons with recent European experience in mind, shrink from the psychological and economic uprooting and suffering that go with a large-scale exchange of population.

The Indian National Congress inevitably regarded the separation of Pakistan from India as a major personal defeat, dangerous in that it might encourage the Indian princes, especially the Nizam of Hyderabad who may look to Pakistan for help, to assert their independence; and therefore it finds difficulty in accustoming itself to the Partition; as its leaders in Bengal have declared, "Congress will work for an undivided Bengal in an undivided India." For some time to come each of the two new Dominions is likely to gird against the other; each is doubtful whether to remain within the British Commonwealth and in these circumstances the weak, unbalanced economic and strategic situation of Pakistan becomes the more dangerous to the peace of India and the world.

The homelands of Pakistan, both in the north-west and north-east, are overwhelmingly agrarian; wheat, cotton, rice and jute being the most valuable crops. Whereas their population of nearly seventy millions forms sixteen per cent of that of all India, their industrial and mineral development, so far as can be judged, cannot amount to more than five per cent of the Indian total, and that, too, obtaining almost wholly in the north-west areas. On the Punjab will fall the main financial strain, for Sind and the North West Frontier Province are deficit provinces, Baluchistan is poor, and East Bengal relatively

INDIA
AND SURROUNDING COUNTRIES

undeveloped. If Pakistan has to maintain unaided the defences of north-west and north-east India on the existing scale, then it can do so only at the expense of the social advance of its people. Pakistan, doubtless, will plan to build mills of its own for cotton and jute, and to protect its products with tariffs; also to develop Chittagong into an alternative port to Calcutta, and Karachi, its new capital, as a rival to Bombay; and later, if finance becomes available, to exploit the great resources of water power in the north-west. But the competing financial and industrial Hindu interests are powerful and these tasks will be difficult of achievement, productive of rivalry and ill-feeling.

All-India mineral resources and raw materials are so distributed as to give economic justification to political unity: cotton and wheat in the north-west and the Deccan, jute and rice in the north-east; coal, iron and mica in Bengal and Bihar, and manganese in the Central Provinces and the south, and it would be tedious to continue. Moreover, the great majority of Hindus and Muslims throughout India are agriculturalists, and in their common interests lies the best hope that one day the lines of communal division in Indian politics may be cut across; but the Partition of India puts back this day by setting a poor, agricultural Muslim state side by side with an industrially strong Hindu India and provocatively poses the issue of agriculture against industry in a communal form.

2. THE DEFENCE OF INDIA

The boundaries of Pakistan are necessarily artificial, denying geography and the work of man. Few lands are so clearly carved by the mountains and the sea to form a single whole as India, and it was largely because the British followed the paths and observed the bounds marked by nature that they so quickly conquered and easily held the country. Separated by 1,000 miles of land and 2,500 miles of sea, the two Muslim states of Pakistan guard the north-west and north-east Indian frontiers, neither impregnable yet both of the first strategic importance. The Second World War demonstrated that only great, united, industrial powers can support total war, only such powers can effectively assert peace. An undivided India might stand in this class, but Pakistan alone disposes neither of the resources in technicians and material nor the defence in depth to protect India: and the threat of atom bomb and germ warfare reinforces this conclusion.

Self-interest, reinforced by India's obligations to the world at large, should dictate a close military alliance between Pakistan and the Indian Union. India's peoples have so long sheltered behind British military and naval strength, and have so much luxuriated in domestic politics, that some considerable time may elapse before they realize that they must bear a world responsibility equal to their numbers and strength. India's own safety is more than India's concern. Geography and history have marked her out as the defensive keystone of the land arch of the Indian Ocean, and all her neighbours rely on her support.

Within India should lie the headquarters of what should become a permanent Indian Ocean defence council, organized within the framework of the United Nations' Organization. Her proper and strategic sphere of interest, first identified by the Portuguese in the sixteenth century and coinciding with the natural expansion of her cultural influence, extends to the entrances of the Indian Ocean; to Singapore, to the Persian Gulf, to Aden and to the Cape of Good Hope. As the last war showed, Burma and Malaya cannot defend themselves by land without the help of India, and the same holds true of her western neighbours, Persia and Afghanistan.

The defeat of Japan and the prolonged conflict in China have placed a clear responsibility on the statesmen of India to give a lead to the countries of Asia. The first Asian Relations Conference, summoned by Pandit Nehru at Delhi in March 1947, strikingly revealed, both in the suspicions of India voiced by the delegates of South-East Asia and in the obvious value of the discussions, the need for such leadership. In order that the responsibilities of Pakistan and the Indian Union should not overstep their power they will need, especially on the sea and in the air, the help of some external power and, as Dominions, their natural ally will be the British Commonwealth, whose

communications converge on India and whose former colony,
Ceylon—now happily also a Dominion—possesses in Trinkomali
the key-port and strategic centre of the Indian Ocean.

In the two World Wars India gave invaluable aid to Britain
and the Allies; in the Second she provisioned the Imperial
forces in Africa, in the Near and Middle East, in South-East
Asia and Australasia: she clothed all the troops east of Suez,
but, more important, under British leadership, she raised the
largest volunteer armies in the world at the rate of 50,000 a
month until they stood at more than two millions strong.

Unfortunately, but inevitably, the magnificent Indian fighting force which still remained after demobilization has been
divided between Pakistan and the Indian Union, first on a
rough and ready basis by moving into the former all Muslim-
majority units and into the latter all exclusively non-Muslim
units and then in a second stage by allowing individual transfers
from the units themselves. Both Dominions properly seek to
create armies composed wholly of Indians officered to the top
by Indians, but, even though Indianization began in 1923 and
under the stress of war increased so rapidly after 1939
that an adequate corps of Indian officers came into service, few
of them by the date of the Partition had reached high rank, and
none higher than Brigadier; and army staffs and commanders
cannot be created overnight. But with British co-operation
and encouragement the difficult interim period need last no
more than a few years. Unfortunately, although presided over
by Lord Mountbatten, the initial Joint Defence Council soon
broke down leaving untouched and unsolved the problem of
the strategic defence of all-India. Certainly to a world just
emerging from total war, the call for a military alliance of
Pakistan and the Indian Union makes sense, if only because
effective defence demands unity.

3 . MASS EDUCATION

The religious gulf between Hindus and Muslims seems too
wide to be bridged; yet a not dissimilar situation existed in
Europe some three hundred years ago. Since that time the
attention of Europeans has been increasingly absorbed by more

universal and fundamental problems, and in this process their religious dissensions, though here and there persisting as in Ireland, have been not so much removed as obscured and dissolved. In the face of difficulties greater than mere religious strife the peoples of Europe came of age. So it should be in Pakistan and the Indian Union for they do not lack problems big enough to frighten and stimulate their peoples. As we have seen, the present religious conflict reflects the deeper political and economic rivalry of Hindu and Muslim middle class groups. More fundamental still, and potentially more threatening to the political and economic health of the world, lies the appalling ignorance and poverty of most Indians, problems which are common to all the states of India.

Above all, India needs universal education. Her total population of some four hundred millions constitutes one-fifth of the world's peoples, and contains one-third of the world's illiterates. In the course of the last century under the British, literacy, namely the ability to read and write a sentence in the vernacular, has increased from four to about twelve per cent, a rate of progress that would give India a literate population some six hundred years hence. However, experiments in Russia and China, and the development in British colonies of new techniques of mass instruction, indicate that a similar result can be achieved in a generation. The British Government in India has already announced far-reaching, expensive plans and the Indian Congress and Muslim League are well aware of the possibilities.

In schemes for mass education, if a quick and lasting advance is to be achieved, all instruction must appear directly relevant to the learners' environment and vocation; and for the 500,000 village communities of India, Mahatma Gandhi's adoption of "basic education," or training through village handicrafts, has pointed the way. For the millions in industry, training on the job and within industry itself forms the most attractive and feasible means of education, and for the tillers of the soil betterment projects allied with literacy campaigns seem to yield the quickest and most satisfactory results.

Behind all Indian education, from primary schools to universities, lies the difficulty, if any sort of cultural integration is to take place, of finding a common language. The spread of English, which can never become universal, has at least shown the unifying influence of a common tongue. Sixteen main languages are spoken in India, but the language called Hindustani, which is in fact not a distinct language but a composite term used to describe the Hindi and Urdu languages, is spoken or understood by a majority of Indians, and is widely accepted as a possible *lingua franca*. It is true that Hindi is favoured by Hindus and Urdu by Muslims but these languages have very much in common. Unfortunately they are written in different scripts: Hindi, which has a Sanskrit base, in what are known as Nagari characters running from left to right; and Urdu, which includes many Persian and Arabic words, in the Persian script from right to left. This difference makes them seem more distinctive than they are in fact, and Hindu-Muslim political rivalry, especially their separate electorates which encouraged separate political platforms and newspapers, promoted this separatism in language.

The Partition of India unfortunately reinforces this tendency, thus adding linguistic to religious and political cleavage. Clearly, if Indian and Pakistan leaders are concerned to promote peace and progress in India, it will be most important for them to see that both scripts are taught in the primary schools, or, better still, to ensure that both languages are written in the Roman script so that their undoubted similarity will appear, and children and men may be drawn together through a common tongue.

In both Pakistan and the Indian Union men outnumber women, and in the bigger cities by as many as two to one. This disparity puts a premium on women as wives and mothers, and partly accounts for their backwardness compared even with their menfolk. Ninety-seven women out of every hundred cannot read or write; thus the dominating influence in the Indian home encourages the perpetuation of custom and opposes change. Social reform therefore comes about slowly. Public opinion, for example, tolerates a desperate state of public health which gives the Indian at birth an expectation of life of only twenty-six years, as compared with the Briton's sixty-two, and only half the Indians born reach the age of twenty-two, instead of nearly seventy as in U.S.A. Sickness is correspondingly widespread: over a quarter of India's peoples suffer from malaria every year; cholera, smallpox, plague, tuberculosis, guinea-worm, yaws and many other diseases take their steady toll of life and health; and breed inefficiency, apathy, poverty and misery.

This gigantic problem does not entirely depend for its solution on better nutrition and the creation of vast numbers of hospitals, nurses, clinics, doctors. These are needed, and in time will come, but the main battle could be joined at once in the home. A general knowledge and application by Indian wives and mothers of the most elementary rules of hygiene would quickly raise the standard of life. Indian women have scarcely begun to look after their own sex. Child marriage persists; infant and maternal mortality rates remain grotesquely high and the struggle for women's emancipation is only just showing results, most noticeably in the abandonment of *purdah* or seclusion.

Caste, the greatest barrier of all, is beginning to give way. It flourished in a parochial economy, but it cannot withstand the denuding effect of Western ideas, of the growth of communications and the mixture of peoples in trains, in buses, in colleges, in industry. A Hindu's choice of occupation grows wider and the limitations on his mixing with members of other castes at meals, for example, less severe. The signs of a social fusion are just visible; the number of inter-caste and inter-religious marriages grows; the movement for the uplift of the depressed classes, sponsored by Mahatma Gandhi, gains ground; and, under self-made leaders like Dr. Ambedkar, they are beginning to strike out for themselves. But what is most needed is a positive social lead from the top: the British as far as possible refrained but the new purely Indian and independent Governments can act more freely and boldly and would be wise to point the moral by setting a target date for the achievement of universal education. The detailed plans for the first five years, prepared on a provincial basis under the guidance of Sir John Sargent, are ready, but inevitably they have been and will be held up by the communal troubles and Partition. Moreover, such plans cannot be carried out cheaply; and to afford them India's peoples must produce more per head. If not, they will remain illiterate, in which event they will also remain poverty-stricken.

In health alone, the application of such plans will ultimately produce standards approximating to those of Britain and U.S.A., but the consequent saving of life will at once focus attention on the greatest problem of all, India's rapidly growing population.

4. POPULATION AND PLANNING

The present rate of population increase is about six millions a year, or some 16,000 a day; and, despite high mortality rates, a total rise of fifteen per cent has taken place over the last decade. Any general improvement in prosperity is quickly reflected in a higher birth-rate; for instance, in the Punjab, the most prosperous province in British India, the official birth-rate was 41 against 34 for All-India. Indian women produce on the average about twice as many children as English women. The spread of birth-control methods constitutes a long-term policy, as does education, especially of women, which alone will ultimately enable the problem to be met. Meanwhile, if public health improves and more food is produced and better distributed, the yearly rate of increase might well become nine millions. The new Dominion Governments therefore must accept an interim policy of constantly providing increasing supplies of food, by home production and import, to satisfy their expanding populations; until the happy day arrives when family limitation relieves them from this, so to speak, persistent chasing of their own tails.

Such a policy concerns not merely agriculture and industry but the whole of Indian development, and is dependent upon the application of modern scientific methods and technology. Russia and U.S.A., especially in the wonderful Tennessee Valley Scheme, have shown how quickly the application of these means can raise the level of national prosperity, and a number of similar plans have already been put forward by Indians. If any such plan is to succeed in India, one criterion certainly applies; as the authors of the famous "Bombay Plan" have declared, "during this period . . . practically every aspect of economic life will have to be so rigorously controlled by Government that individual liberty and freedom of enterprise will suffer a temporary eclipse"; and during their brief presence together in the interim Government both the National Congress and Muslim League showed themselves to be strongly in favour of a vigorously applied planned economy. Such a policy could be carried through only with the support of most Indians, and is therefore feasible for a purely Indian Government; but no Government for which Britain was even partly responsible could have faced its consequences; and in the circumstances the Viceroy in 1944 made the best possible start by setting up a new Department of Planning and Development and placing Sir Ardeshir Dalal at its head. The latter formed an ideal choice: a scientist and civil servant wise enough to appreciate that there are some things which cannot be measured; a Director since 1931 of the Tata Iron and Steel Company, whose Jamshedpur steelworks are the largest in the British Commonwealth, his experience and grasp of large-scale planning were unequalled. Under him general plans were announced for the nationalization of all "basic industries of national importance" and the separate fields of activity for Government and private enterprise demarcated.

But, in the light of the change in 1947 from a British to Indian Governments, these decisions are significant only in relation to the proposals contained in a "Plan of Economic Development for India" published at the beginning of 1944 by a group of eight Indian industrialists, of whom Sir Ardeshir Dalal was one. All of them were either supporters of the Congress or strongly nationalist in their outlook. Their "Bombay Plan," as it is popularly called, was not the first or only Indian plan to appear —a National Planning Committee under Pandit Nehru, for example, led the way by publishing reports on behalf of the Congress in 1939—but it forms the most comprehensive analysis of the subject, and the most likely basis for all such future schemes in Hindu-dominated India, that is to say in the Indian Union as distinct from Pakistan. In the latter a grave lack of capital, of equipment, of material resources and industrial experience is likely long to hold up development.

Declaring that "the maintenance of the economic unity

of India is . . . an essential condition of any effective planning," the "Bombay Plan" assumes the existence of an All-India Federation and a central directing authority. Broadly, it seeks to achieve for Indians a minimum standard of living in terms of nutrition, clothing, house-room, education and health services, and proposes to attain this within fifteen years by doubling India's national income per head, which, allowing for the growth of population to about 490 millions by 1960, would require in practice a threefold increase on the 1939 average income level of some £5 yearly.

This, it is estimated, can be achieved by doubling agricultural production, trebling the main services, and increasing the industrial output five-fold, which would still leave India's economy mainly agricultural but more balanced than at present. The plan assumes development in three five-year stages in the first of which priority is to be given to the creation of basic industries, especially power in the form of electricity, for the production of capital goods. In agriculture the peasants, whose average scattered holdings of about three acres are incontestably too small for profitable working, will be compelled to farm co-operatively; rural indebtedness, which at present breaks the peasant's heart, is to be eliminated through co-operative credit societies partly financed by the State; and the modern techniques of irrigation, afforestation, manuring and mechanization increasingly used to grow more food; meanwhile the peasant farmer is to be educated and at the same time stimulated by the creation in all areas of model farms.

The authors expect that these and many other auxiliary projects will cost in the first fifteen years 10,000 crores of rupees (£7,500,000,000) at the 1931–39 values, a figure which in terms of present-day prices is likely to be nearer 20,000 crores. It is suggested that the money can be raised through internal savings, sterling balances, foreign loans and, lastly, what the Plan calls "created money," which amounts to about one-third of the total. The danger of inflating India's already rising cost of living is real, as the authors have recognized, and it is unlikely that for the amounts quoted they will be able to provide the whole of the social services proposed. Their attention, in fact, is concentrated rather on labour and materials than on finance and, as they deliberately state, their estimates of expenditure are "to be regarded merely as rough approximations and their value as more illustrative than absolute."

Superficially, the "Bombay Plan" has drawn on the experience of Russia's five-year experiments; but the essential of Russia's plans was the cutting down of consumption for capital expenditure. India, however, enjoys no such margin from which to afford this. Over the Russian five-year plans, too, the State from the beginning exercised and did not hesitate to use full power, but the "Bombay Plan" trusts rather that its aims can be achieved by consent in the first place, and that the State's powers of control shall gradually increase during the period of planning; and yet its proposals imply from the start the application of rationing, price controls, heavy taxation, and a high level of savings.

In short, it contains many contradictions and its generalizations are based on hopes rather than on facts. But it has been more widely read by Indians than any other social document of recent years, catching their imagination and carrying their interest to a high pitch. Essentially the Plan forms a statement of aims which has opened new vistas to Indian minds. Therein lies its greatest importance, and henceforth no Government in India is likely to dare in its social and economic policy to seek less. The Plan, which was a product of Hindu minds and a revelation of the mighty power of Hindu financial and industrial groups, confirmed Muslims in their belief that in a united India they would be permanently subordinated not only politically, but economically and culturally, too. Its publication reinforced their determination to achieve Pakistan, albeit on a lower standard of living, and with it a greater degree of political and economic freedom.

5. THE ECONOMIC AND SOCIAL FUTURE

Undeterred by the war and the politicians' prolonged failure to reach agreement, the sponsors of the "Bombay Plan" set about putting their grand design into practice. A group of them, led by Mr. G. D. Birla, the great Marwari financier and industrialist and friend of Mahatma Gandhi, visited both

Britain and U.S.A. in 1944, seeking and gaining promises for the post-war supply not merely of capital equipment but also, and equally important, of blueprints, formulas and technicians. Amply justifying their confidence, India's industrial and financial assets mounted at a truly astonishing rate. Most important of all, Britain, the country whose co-operation was essential, had become indebted to India by 1946 to the tune of some £1,300 millions, an amount considerably greater, for instance, than the whole of the loan made by U.S.A. to tide Britain over her post-war economic difficulties. Broadly speaking, this vast debt had piled up during the war because Britain had undertaken to repay all money expended in India on Imperial as distinct from purely local defence; in this manner handsomely making amends for the earlier, unfair policy of using India's forces as a kind of Imperial reserve solely at India's expense.

The close of the war therefore found India both better equipped and disposing of greater financial resources for future development than ever before in her history.

The bulk of India's monetary claims on Britain, or sterling balances as they are generally termed, can be repaid only through the export of British goods and services to India; and such a large burden can hardly be discharged in much less than a generation. Presumably the balances will be divided between Pakistan and the Indian Union, and the commercial links forged by their past associations with Britain, interlocked by their complementary economies, should thus be strengthened by their mutually developing policies. Already in the first six months of 1946 British exports to India exceeded by over a hundred per cent the 1938 figure of £17 millions, and India's exports to Britain were up by twenty per cent on the 1938 figure of £25 millions.

Each country already bids fair to become the other's best customer in circumstances more conducive to friendly relations than ever before. Pakistan needs Britain's capital and help in her industrial development. A politically independent Indian Union asks for not as in the past cheap cotton goods, which she is well able to produce herself, but heavy machinery and vehicles, including locomotives, electrical and scientific instruments, chemicals and dye-stuffs and non-ferrous manufactures. In short, she is entering upon the second phase in her own industrial revolution and, as the standard of living of her people rises, she will undoubtedly buy more of the best manufactures of Britain. At the same time she is easily able to supply in raw materials Britain's main demands, especially mica, linseed, castor oils, and hides. India's wartime loss of Japanese and European markets was and is balanced by a growth of trade with U.S.A. which in value rivals that with Britain and is certain to increase. By virtue of her present trading importance India has been granted a permanent seat on the governing body of the International Monetary Fund; and during the next quarter-century her exports and imports are likely to rise substantially, which is as it should be, for a sub-continent containing twenty per cent of the world's population ought properly to absorb more than her present five per cent of the world's total trade.

Only sixteen per cent of the population of India live in towns of more than 5,000 people, and therefore to-day, as throughout her history, the countryside not the towns, farming and food production and not industry, remain the centre of gravity of Indian life for the majority of Hindus and Muslims. With the largest cattle population, she stands as the chief supplier of skins and hides in the world; she produces more sugar than any other country; and in cotton and jute realizes valuable cash crops. Indeed, with a wide range of climate—from the rice and rubber-producing lands of the far south to the wheat and coniferous forests of the Punjab and Himalayas—India can grow the widest selection of products of which soil is capable.

Although India's external trade remains predominatingly that of a country producing raw materials, she ranks among the first eight industrial powers in the world, a position she has assumed largely through the demands and opportunities of two World Wars. In the interval between them her growth was disappointingly slow, probably because, under the Government of India Act of 1919, industrial policy devolved on the provinces, which disposed of neither the resources nor experience to pursue active development schemes; and, for example, of the expansion between 1921 and 1939 nearly one-third actually took place within the Indian states where taxation generally was lower.

In the closing stages of the Second World War India's industrial advance again became marked. By 1946 she was turning out most of the equipment required by a modern mechanized army and beginning to make her own railway materials, including locomotives. Soon after the war ended a national aircraft industry was started at Bangalore with a twenty-year target of complete self-sufficiency, and a beginning was made in creating motor-car and shipbuilding industries. She has simultaneously developed what is claimed to be the second largest film industry in the world. Lack of power in the form of electricity at present hinders manufacturing development but, if present plans mature, her water resources, almost equal to those of Canada and U.S.A., will be harnessed to fill this need. Even so, in her basic industries she already produces more coal, more iron and more steel than any other country in the Commonwealth except Britain. Undoubtedly, India's economic development has been held back by the communal fighting and disorders, and orderly progress will be hindered by the Partition itself, but so determined is the urge to industrialize among the powerful Indian political and economic groups that it cannot altogether be gainsaid.

Most Indian industry is owned and managed by Indians, particularly by those great groups of castes who have long held among Hindus the monopoly of commercial and industrial pursuits. Inevitably, the much poorer Muslim community resents and fears the economic as much as the political power of the Hindus, but of equal importance for India's future development is the fact that large scale industry has engendered a countrywide, working class movement transcending merely communal and caste divisions, and possessing in unsatisfactory working and often dreadful living conditions a powerful motive for common action. Already over two hundred and fifty recognized Trade Unions have been formed, including a number whose sympathies lie with the rapidly-growing Communist party, and attempts have been and are being made to create all-India federations of unions. Equally significant is the emergence of lower middle class groups, consisting of the army of clerical staffs of business houses, banks and Government offices, just beginning to realize that they have interests in common: sober, respectable folk earning between £5 and £15 a month, and many of them graduates of Indian universities. Slowly, even though it has been obscured by communal antagonisms—and will be hindered by the Partition —a fresh stratification of Indian society is taking place: local, perpendicularly divided groups begin to give way to broader, countrywide and horizontal layers of society. New all-India industrial classes evolve to balance the long established upper middle classes and the more narrowly based capitalist groups. The pattern of India's future society begins to emerge, and with it a grammar of politics in which Hindu-Muslim and other sect rivalries will be caught up in the growing self-consciousness, in the conflicts and in the creative syntheses of countrywide classes.

India's deeper problems, which throw into perspective the communal rivalries of to-day, are so challenging and the means of solution so nearly within grasp as to stimulate the best will and work of Indians, whether Hindu or Muslim. Political independence gives them for the first time in centuries the opportunity to be and to know themselves, to shed their strong sense of humiliation and to achieve a new confidence; the opportunity, too, of so re-creating their civilizations and countries as to bring in the East to redress the Western balance of the world. In these circumstances, the proper attitude of mind of Europeans and Americans towards India is not difficult to determine. If we are mindful of the persisting divisions and dissensions among the folk of our own continents, we shall not expect the more numerous Indian peoples quickly to provide complete remedies for their own political, economic and social ills: we shall neither protest our goodwill nor rashly proffer our counsel, but rather make up our minds to give to Indians what they most need, our friendship and understanding.

STATISTICS OF POPULATION AND COMMUNITIES

TABLE I

INDIA: POPULATION 1941

	Males	Females	Total
British India.	153,045,000	142,782,000	295,809,000
States and Agencies	47,883,000	45,090,000	93,189,000
Total	200,928,000	187,872,000	388,998,000

TABLE II

INDIA: PRINCIPAL COMMUNITIES, 1941

(Figures are given in thousands)

Province or State	Hindus other than scheduled castes	Scheduled Castes	Muslims	Christians	Sikhs	Total
Madras . .	34,731	8,068	3,896	2,047	·4	49,342
Bombay. .	14,700	1,855	1,920	375	8	20,850
Bengal . .	17,680	7,379	33,005	166	16	60,307
U.P. . .	34,095	11,717	8,416	160	232	55,021
Punjab . .	6,302	1,249	16,217	505	3,757	28,419
Bihar . .	22,174	4,340	4,716	35	13	36,340
C.P. . .	9,881	3,051	784	59	15	16,814
Assam . .	3,537	676	3,442	41	3	10,205
N.W.F.P. .	180	—	2,789	11	58	3,038
Orissa . .	5,595	1,238	146	28	·2	8,729
Sind . .	1,038	192	3,208	20	31	4,535
Total, British India . .	150,890	39,921	79,399	3,482	4,165	295,809
Hyderabad .	10,382	2,928	2,097	220	5	16,339
Mysore . .	5,282	1,405	485	113	·3	7,329
Travancore .	3,146	396	434	1,960	—	6,070
Kashmir .	694	113	3,074	4	66	4,022
Gwalior .	3,463	—	241	2	2	4,006
Baroda . .	1,963	231	224	9	·6	2,855
Total, States * and Agencies	55,227	8,892	12,660	2,834	1,526	93,189
Total, India† .	206,117	48,813	92,058	6,317	5,691	388,998

*The six states that appear here are those with the largest population.

†According to the Government of Pakistan its estimated population in 1948 is 65·6 millions of whom 23·8 millions are in Western Pakistan (18·2 millions Muslims) and 41·8 millions in Eastern Pakistan (29·6 millions Muslims).

NOTE ON BOOKS

The following brief list of books is suggested to readers who wish to pursue further the subjects dealt with in this volume.

GENERAL:

The Cambridge Shorter History of India, ed. H. Dodwell. (Cambridge, 1934.)

Majumdar, R. C., Raychaudhuri, H. C., Datta, K.: *An Advanced History of India*. (London, 1946.)

(Parts I and II of the *Advanced History* and Part III of the *Cambridge Shorter History* together form an admirable outline.)

EARLY INDIA:

Raychaudhuri, H. C.: *Political History of Ancient India*. (Calcutta, 1923.)

Smith, V. A.: *Asoka*. (Oxford, 1901.)

Beni Prasad: *The State in Ancient India*. (Allahabad, 1928.)

O'Malley, L. S. S.: *Indian Caste Customs*. (Cambridge, 1932.)

MUSLIM INDIA:

Iswari Prasad: *Medieval India*. (Allahabad, 1925.)

Smith, V. A.: *Akbar the Great Mogul*. (Oxford, 1917.)

Sarkar, J.: *Mughal Administration*. (Calcutta, 1920.)

Moreland, W. H.: *India at the Death of Akbar*. (London, 1920.)

Moreland, W. H.: *India from Akbar to Aurangzeb*. (London, 1923.)

Sardesai, G. S.: *Main Currents of Maratha History*. (Bombay, 1933.)

THE EUROPEAN COMPANIES:

Whiteway, R. S.: *Rise of the Portuguese Power in India*. (London, 1899.)

Lannoy, C., and Linder, H.: *L'Expansion Coloniale des Peuples Européens*. (Brussels, 1907.)

Dodwell, H.: *Dupleix and Clive*. (London, 1920.)

Hickey, W.: *Memoirs*, ed. A. Spencer. (London, 1919–25.)

Moon, P.: *Warren Hastings*. (London, 1947.)

Roberts, P. E.: *India Under Wellesley*. (London, 1929.)

Philips, C. H.: *The East India Company*. (Manchester, 1940.)

Thompson, E. : *The Making of the Indian Princes*. (Oxford, 1943.)

Muir, R. (ed.) : *The Making of British India*. (Manchester, 1915.)

(This work includes a most useful series of extracts from primary authorities on the history of the East India Company.)

MODERN INDIA :

Lee Warner, Sir W. : *The Native States of India*. (London, 1910.)

Davies, C. C. : *The North West Frontier*. (Cambridge, 1932.)

Panikkar, K. M. : *India and the Indian Ocean*. (London, 1945.)

Wint, G. : *The British in Asia*. (London, 1947.)

Brayne, F. L. : *Socrates in an Indian Village*. (London, 1929.)

Hartog, Sir P. : *Some Aspects of Indian Education Past and Present*. (London, 1939.)

A Plan of Economic Development for India. (London, 1945.)

The Montagu-Chelmsford Report. Cmd. 9109 of 1928.

The Simon Commission Report. Cmd. 3568 of 1930.

Beni Prasad : *Hindu-Muslim Questions*. (London, 1946.)

Gandhi, M. K. : *Mahatma Gandhi ; His Own Story*, ed. C. F. Andrews. (London, 1930.)

Nehru, J. : *An Autobiography*. (London, 1936.)

Nehru, J. : *The Discovery of India*. (London, 1946.)

Coupland, Sir R. : *Report on the Constitutional Problem in India*. Parts I, II and III. (Oxford, 1942–43.)

(These three detailed studies are summed up in the same author's *India : A Restatement*. (Oxford, 1945.)

Detailed bibliographies will be found in the various volumes of *The Cambridge History of India*.

INDEX